Maker's Mindset

The Maker's Mindset:

A Practical Philosophy for Building Things That Matter

ISBN: 979-8-9943838-0-3

Initial print in the United States

First Trade size Printing Feburary, 2026

Presented by

Beard Iron Books & Thomas Burbridge, M.Ed.

That teacher who assigns homework over winter vacation.

Bwhahahahahahaha!

THE MAKER'S MINDSET

A Practical Philosophy for Building Things That Matter

THOMAS BURBRIDGE M.ED.

Illustrations by Hannabee

For Brigette, without you, my path would not be clear.

This page is suspitiously left blank

Thank your local finfoil hat wearer for this service.

A Very Strange Forward

Consuela—at least the name I believe she gave me, slid into the chair across from mine just as my Huevos a la Mexicana arrived, still sizzling.

It was hot enough to demand attention. Instead, I gave it none. I told her about my book. I showed her the page where I thanked her business by name. She smiled, nodded—and then she began to talk.

She spoke of fifth-grade education. Of arriving in the United States in the 1960s, of becoming a citizen, of three failed businesses before spending her last few thousand dollars on a small taco stand at the corner of Railroad and Pecan.

El Rincón or for those who forget that the P is silent in Pflugerville, It is the corner in English.

She did not romanticize about her upbringings, the once proud marriage, but what she did tell me was a story about grit. Married at sixteen. Divorced at twenty-seven. She spoke of her staff the way others speak of family. She shaped them into her way of running a Mexican food restaurant—not through manuals or management theory, but through example. She gave people work when they needed it. She treated them as her own.

They returned the favor with fierce loyalty.

More than five of her employees, by my count, have worked beside her for thirty-five years. Her small corner restaurant carries more combined experience than the local police force.

She mentioned, almost apologetically, that she still wished she had earned her GED. As she spoke, a thought settled quietly and refused to leave.

Education creates opportunity but so does grit and tenacity.

She had learned that as a single mother of five. By doing the work. By doing it wrong. By doing it again until it was right. I realized it wasn't education she lacked, nor even education she truly wanted. It was the marker. The quiet satisfaction of holding credentials that say finished, even when the work itself had been complete for decades.

I've been coming to El Rincon since moving to Pflugerville in 2015. What she learned by doing—by risking real money, feeding real people, and standing by those who stood by her—barely appears in business school textbooks.

She left me with cold eggs and refried beans while I scratched a few notes onto a Post-it pad stuck inside my laptop.
I didn't mind. Her restaurant does not run on policy, theory, or credentials.

There was a moment when I wanted to relay to Consuela about the mindset rules I spent so many months scratching out on her tables, but I didn't need to and I left that day wishing that I could add one more Mindset rule to the book: Have Grit. Consuela was the proof I needed to validate my claims. She is the epitome of Grit.

Maker's Mindset

Postscript

If you find yourself in Pflugerville Texas, visit El Rincón. Ask for the Verde salsa with chips. The pozole soup is worth the pause.

When you see a hopped-up Electric Bike out front, stop in and say 'Hi', I'll be at a table somewhere writing my next adventure.

~tb

Nothing to see here…move along.

Maker's Mindset

INSIDE THIS BOOK

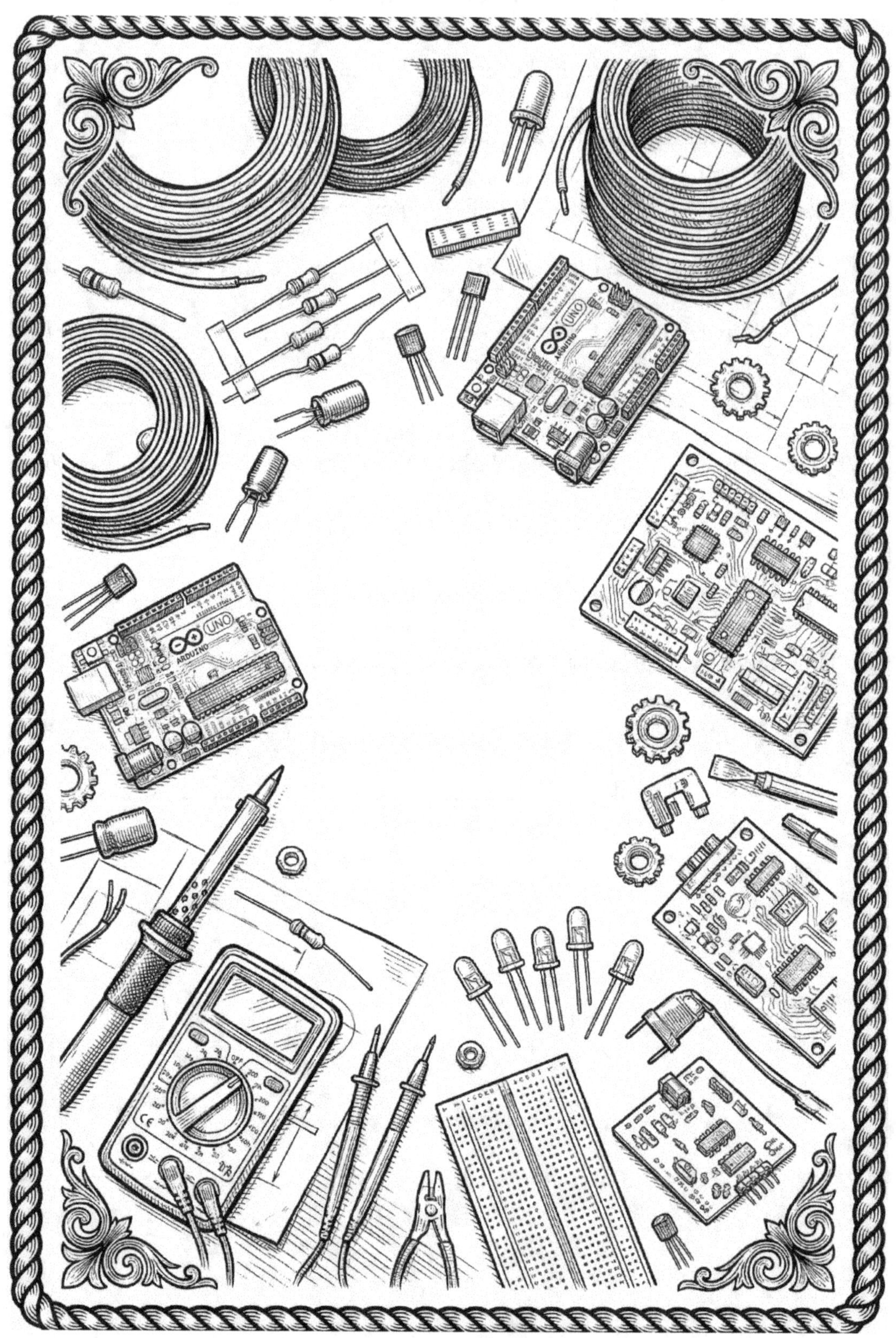

About this book

This book is not a manual or a curriculum guide. It is a way of thinking, one built from classrooms, workshops, failed prototypes, close calls, and moments where curiosity almost died but didn't.

What This Book Is Not

- This is not a step-by-step how-to manual.
- This is not a STEM-only textbook.
- This is not motivational fluff built on empty slogans.

This book is a mindset guide; meant to be lived, tested, argued with, and adapted.

What Is a Maker?

In this book, a maker is not defined by tools, job titles, or technical skill. A maker is anyone who looks at the world and asks, "How does this work?" and then takes responsibility for improving it. Makers can be students, teachers, engineers, artists, parents, or retirees. They build with their hands, their minds, and their communities. What unites them is not what they make, but how they think: curious, resourceful, resilient, and unwilling to accept "that's just how it is" as a final answer.

The Maker's Mindset is written for teachers, students, tinkerers, engineers, leaders, and anyone who builds things with other humans. The setting doesn't matter. The mindset does. You won't find step-by-step instructions for every problem here. What you will find is a framework for how makers think, work, fail, recover, and succeed together. This book is organized around ten mindset rules, but they are not independent rules. They function as a system. When one rule is ignored, the others weaken. When one rule is strengthened, the rest become easier to live by. Safety supports experimentation. Reflection sharpens judgment. Community multiplies skill. Tools extend intent. None of this work alone for very long. There is also an unspoken force running through every chapter: fear. Fear doesn't usually look dramatic. It doesn't announce itself. It shows up quietly, as silence in a room full of people, as tools left unused, as ideas dismissed too quickly, as students who stop raising their hands, or teams that stop trusting each other. Fear breaks toolboxes long before anything physically shatters. The Maker's Mindset is not about eliminating fear. That's impossible. It's about recognizing it, understanding how it distorts judgment, and designing environments, classrooms, teams, and communities where curiosity is stronger than hesitation. You'll see stories here. Some are funny. Some are uncomfortable. All of them are real in the way that matters. They exist to illustrate a simple truth: progress doesn't come from flawless plans or perfect people. It comes from thoughtful risk, shared responsibility, and the courage to try again with better awareness than last time. If you're looking for permission to break rules, this isn't that book. If you're looking for permission to think, question, build, fail, reflect, and grow, within a system designed to support you when things go wrong.

Classroom Beginnings

Greetings, and Thank You!

This book began in the trenches of a middle school classroom sometime around 2016. At the time, I was locked in a passionate debate with a very determined, perhaps overly confident, eighth grader. The topic? Design.

She insisted, (quite adamantly), that the fashion of creation must come first. It had to be pretty. It had to sparkle. Rainbows, unicorns, bubbles, the whole aesthetic package. She was designing a birdhouse for a 3D printer and wanted it to be an Instagram-ready masterpiece.

I, on the other hand, made a case for something radically different: functionality.

"Pretty doesn't always fly. But function? That lands every time."

Before we get too deep, let me say this: If you're reading this and you're a classroom teacher, bless you. Truly. Use this book as a guide. Each one of these mindset rules has been developed by opening young minds to new possibilities. It's my intention to plant several seeds that help our kids grow.

If you're a reader who loves building, making, or any form of engineering, this book is your launchpad. Use these ideas as a foundational step toward your goals. Some of the mindsets speak directly to working in teams (always a challenge), so I've included one called Use Your Tools. You'll understand why that's essential soon enough.

Back to that birdhouse.

I held my ground and scribbled a simple formula on the whiteboard:

Function = Something That Works

Fashion = Something That Looks Good

She rolled her eyes. I shrugged. Then, I did the hardest thing a teacher can do: I let her try.

She gave it all. She did her best to make "pretty" work. And when it came time to present her design to a panel of her peers, her glittery, impractical birdhouse, with its tiny decorative fridge, a bird-sized television, and a spiral slide, was kindly but firmly rejected in favor of a more realistic, utilitarian model. One that could house a bird. Preferably without the bird-sized Netflix subscription.

Maker's Moment

Let your learners fail forward. Failure to do well is just research in disguise. The sooner we learn what doesn't work, the sooner we find what does.

As it turns out, birds don't care about aesthetics. They care about shelter, safety, and a soft place to build a nest. They don't need architecture inspired by Pinterest. They need purpose-built simplicity. And in that moment, my student learned what I now consider one of the greatest truths in making:

Maker's Mindset

"Experience is a better teacher than I'll ever be."[1]

That moment, that humbling, humorous, and oh-so-human moment stayed with me. It wasn't just a teaching win. It was a seed. That seed that grew into this book.

What started as a single skirmish over practicality versus appearance eventually evolved into something much bigger: a way of thinking. A mindset. One that values failure, celebrates function, embraces messy learning, and invites everyone, especially the stubborn ones, to roll up their sleeves and make something that matters.

Pro tip for Makers: Function first.

It's easy to get caught up in appearance, but it's just decoration if something doesn't work. So here we are, The Maker's Mindset. A book forged in hot glue, broken circuits, half-finished projects, and much trial and error.

Changing Mindsets: Advice for adults.

Changing one's mindset, especially toward adopting a maker's mindset, involves deliberate practice and intentional shifts in perspective.

A Note to Fellow Educators

If you're an educator or classroom teacher using this book as a guide for students, bless you. Truly. May you succeed in your work and find joy in your students' growth. This work isn't easy; anyone who tells

---

[1] There are those who use the word 'Failure' as a weapon. These are the people who, 1. Either imprint their own fear of failure on others or, 2. Have never accepted their own failures and, 3. Never separated people from the process.

you otherwise hasn't stood in their shoes. Here are a few words of wisdom from someone who has been in the arena:

Expect closed mindsets.

Expect students to shut down when things don't work. I once had a student call herself pathetic at the end of the year because she couldn't build a remote-controlled robot car. She'd internalized the failure so profoundly that she just closed up muttering something about being severely disciplined at home and being grounded for two lifetimes. I handed her a Pringles can, floral tape, a few peanut-butter jar lids and some rubber bands. "Now," I said in my strictest possible teacher voice. "Build it wrong." I instructed her to give her a 30-minute time limit. "None of it can be right – it all has to be wrong."

I turned from her as she struggled to close her mouth, then with a spark in her eye, she did exactly what I instructed.

If you're a teacher, you will recognize this technique for breaking closed mindsets. For the rest of the world, what I did with this student was force her to build something that she most feared[2].

Allow exploration.

Don't limit makers with rigid rules. At the start of the year, I ask my students to build a structure that supports the weight of a coffee cup. Then I sip from ridiculous mugs while threatening them with extra homework if I spill. On Judgment Day, I dress like a judge and slam down

---

[2] Fear has no place in my classroom. By asking her to do something positive with what she knew what was going to fail, she is succeeding at failing. Breaking the cycle of fear.

a yoga ball that weighs the same as a Trenta coffee from Starbucks. Because expectations shift, and so should our designs.

Value the process over the grade.

Some students cheat or use shortcuts to get an A. I tell them straight: "If you want the A that bad, I'll give it to you right now. Final grade: A. But for all ten check-in grades before that? Zeros." The learning isn't in the letter. It's in the making.

Treat the engineering notebook like scripture.

This is their personal lab manual, blueprint archive, and journal of innovation. If they take it seriously, they'll start seeing patterns in their thinking. Make it sacred.

Use great resources.

Subscribe to or dig into Popular Mechanics, Make: Magazine, The MagPi, and Nuts & Volts. Explore Tinkercad for modeling. Sites like makeworld.com, thingiverse.com, and yeggi.com are treasure troves for makers.

Most important: HAVE FUN.

Teaching can be brutal. Between IEPs, 504s, teenage drama, disruptive behaviors, and being told you're doing everything wrong by administrators, it's easy to burn out. Fun is your shield. Let it live in your classroom. Let it be your rebellion. Your students will feel it. They'll rise with you.

Importance of the right teaching tool

The Advantages of 3D Printing in Education

If there is one machine that exemplifies the maker mindset of rapid learning, fast failures, and glorious experimentation it is the 3D printer. None of the tools in a classroom lab bridge the gap between imagination and physical reality quite like this one. Students can think, model, and hold it in their hands, all within a single class period. When it comes to reliability and classroom toughness, I lean hard on the Elegoo Neptune 4 Pro.

A 3D printer needs to be more than good-looking or hyped up with influencer ads. It must survive the daily gauntlet of curious hands, bumped tables, spaghetti failures, and the occasional spilled water bottle. The Neptune 4 Pro is sturdy, dependable, and easy to service, making it my go-to recommendation over many of the more popular. If a printer can survive 26 teenagers poking, jostling, and hovering around it while asking, "Can I print mine now?", then its battle tested.

However, a printer is only as good as its software and design pipeline. That's where Tinkercad comes in. This free, browser-based CAD tool is brilliant for beginners and seasoned tinkerers. Tinkercad allows students to learn design thinking principles, understanding volume, symmetry, spacing, and constraints while giving them immediate visual feedback. Tinkercad isn't just a tool; it's an interactive sketchpad for innovation.

Students start by solving a real-world problem or reimagining an existing product. With Tinkercad, they model their concept in 3D space, which teaches not only spatial reasoning and geometry but also engineering logic: How will this fit? Can it print? Will it break?

Maker's Mindset

These kinds of questions push students from passive learners to active problem solvers.

Once their designs are complete, the 3D printer becomes their feedback loop. Students get to watch their ideas materialize, layer by layer, failure by failure, success by success. This is where the concept of rapid prototyping enters the scene. With 3D printing, iteration becomes part of the workflow. Something doesn't fit. Redesign it. Print it again. Adjust. Improve.

Each cycle is a lesson in resilience, precision, and patience, all crucial engineering habits.

The classroom shifts from lecture-based learning to a mini design firm. Students stop asking, "What's the right answer?" and start asking, "What else can I try?" That shift is monumental.

Final Thoughts

3D printing in the classroom especially with tools like the Elegoo Neptune 4 Pro and Tinkercad removes the line between student and inventor. It gives every learner a shot at physical creation. It's one thing to teach theoretical design, it's another to let a kid hold their idea in their hand. That's when the learning sticks.

And that's the essence of the Maker's Mindset.

A Note to Student Tinkerers

If you're a student who builds things with your hands, curiosity, and a bit of chaos, welcome to the maker's club. This is where your ideas grow wild, failures become mentors, and inventions begin.

From someone who's been there:

1. Safety First, Second, and Always.

Before you power it, cut, drill, melt, or test it, pause. Ask yourself: is this safe? Do I have goggles on? Are my fingers clear? Is this thing going to explode or burn me? It's not fun to end a project with a trip to the nurse or worse. Safety isn't boring, it's smart.

2. You will mess up. A lot.

Wires cross. Batteries short or die. Things catch fire (hopefully in simulation). That's how you learn. Mistakes are part of engineering, just like screws and solder.

3. Build it wrong to build it right.

If you're afraid of doing it wrong, you'll never do it at all. Try the bad version. Make a mess. Then figure out what didn't work, and why. That's how pros learn, too.

4. Respect your tools.

Know how to use a Dremel before turning it on. Learn how to hold a soldering iron so you don't burn yourself. Tools are powerful, they can create or destroy.

Take care of them and they'll take care of you.

5. Document everything.

Use your engineering notebook like it's a logbook for an explorer. Write down your ideas, sketch your designs, and record every test, even the failures. This becomes your map through creative chaos.

6. Don't fear the ugly prototype.

Maker's Mindset

Your first version will be ugly, wobbly, and full of tape. That's version one. Version two is better, and version three is amazing. Great things start rough.

7. Ask questions. Use your mentors.

Ask your teacher, classmates, online forums, and your weird uncle who knows how to weld. Makers are a tribe, and we share knowledge freely. You're never alone.

8. Most of all: Have fun.

Engineering is complex, but it should still feel like magic. Be silly. Build something just to make your friends laugh. Hack a pencil sharpener into a bubble machine. Play. Tinkering is learning disguised as chaos.

Stay safe. Stay curious. Stay weird. Keep tinkering.

Note to Teachers:

Educators often want to front-load students with knowledge, lists, posters, slide decks, and well-rehearsed lectures. However, when it comes to teaching mindsets, none stick like lived experience. Mindsets aren't absorbed through observation alone, they're shaped by doing, failing, adjusting, and trying again.

You can hang a beautifully laminated sign that says "Growth Mindset" on your classroom wall, but it will never have the same impact as a student who just rebuilt their failed project and saw it finally working.

That moment teaches more than any quote ever could. If you want your students to value perseverance, let them wrestle with a problem until they find a solution. Let them lead the safety briefing if you want them to adopt a safety-first mindset. If you want them to respect tools, let them break a dull drill bit, then show them how to fix it.

Teaching mindsets requires trust. Trust that students can handle the challenges. Trust that some will fail. Trust that your job is not to prevent failure but to ensure it's safe, educational, and recoverable.

In short: Mindsets are best learned through struggle, success, and story, not slides. So, take a step back.

Allow students to wrestle with the work. Stay present, guide with questions, and celebrate the process, not just the outcome. This is how makers are made.

The Tribe of Makers – Teachers, Tinkerers, and Students.

There are many paths into the maker's world. Some enter through the classroom, others through garage doors and back sheds. Some stumble in after breaking the lawnmower. Others march in proudly, cradling a soldering iron like a sword. But once you're here, you're one of us. This chapter is for the tribe.

Whether you teach, tinker, or learn by doing, you belong.

For the teachers who sacrifice prep periods to sort through boxes of parts, turn outdated equipment into curriculum gold, and tell a student, **"Try it again, but break it this time on purpose."**

For the self-taught engineers who build prototypes from pickle jars and scrap plywood, keep burnt components in a shoebox as trophies, and know the deep joy of hearing something clicks into place after 40 hours of failure.

Maker's Mindset

And for the students, the brave, the unsure, the wild thinkers, who dare to pick up tools before they know what they're doing. You are the future of this world. We don't need perfect students. We need curious ones. We need you.

Degrees, titles, or certifications don't define the tribe of makers. It's characterized by grit. By failure. By the tenacity to say, "That didn't work, but here's what I learned." It's a tribe that knows full well that progress does not come from flawless plans but from the courage to try anyway.

Safety is not optional; it's the first skill. Before innovation comes self-preservation. Safety isn't about slowing you down, it's about keeping you in the game long enough to change it. No one earns respect by ignoring safety.

Respect your tools, your materials, and your body. You only get one set of organic hands. 3D printing another set is tedious, cumbersome and time consuming.

Documentation is your secret weapon. Engineers write. Makers sketch. Students scribble. Keep your notebook. Track the process. Every mistake, every hunch, every half-baked idea might be the key to your next big insight. And when you finally get it to work, you'll want to know how you did it.

If it's not written down, it doesn't happen. Your notebook is your second brain.

Celebrate your first versions. No one's first attempt looks good. Embrace the janky prototype. Clap for the mess. Laugh at the failures, because they mean you're building. Most people never even try. You did. **Ugly is the first draft of amazing.**

Use your community. Your community is your ambulance. Your mentors, your classmates, your online forums, your retired machinist neighbors are potential sparks. Talk to them. Share. Ask. Teach. This tribe grows stronger when it grows together.

Knowledge shared is power multiplied.

Have fun. Always, always have fun. Yes, this work is hard. But joy is fuel. Tinkering is freedom. There is wonder in seeing your idea move, light up, or even just not fall apart. Even in frustration, there is something beautiful about caring enough to keep trying.

If you're not smiling at least once per building, you're doing it wrong.

The Maker's Mindset is not a rulebook. It's a spark. Whether in a classroom, a warehouse, a kitchen, or a cardboard fort you turned into a lab, this mindset is yours. Own it. Break stuff. Document your journey. Share your failures. Celebrate your wins.

We are all still learning. Always.

Welcome to the tribe. Thank you for picking it up. I hope you find some wisdom, laughter, and the courage to make something bold.

Let's get started.

It's too quiet on this page. Turn and find another.

MINDSET RULE ZERO
SAFETY IS
PARAMOUNT

Mindset Rule Zero

Safety is Paramount

Parents touring my classroom always ask the same question. So do my rule-followers, the ones who highlight every step of a lab with color-coded notes and triple-check their procedures. They're bright, careful, and wonderfully curious:

"Why is safety Rule Zero? Why not Rule One?"

Because nothing comes before zero. Mindset Rule Zero is the foundation, the space between thought and action, the breath before the spark. You must be safe before you create, before you build, before you even begin to imagine what's possible.

Safety as a State of Being

Safety isn't a checklist or a laminated poster. It's a way of thinking. It's not just what you do when someone's watching; it's who you are when no one is.

Policies can be followed mindlessly. Mindsets cannot. To live with a Safety Mindset is to live aware. You notice where your hands are, where others are standing, where energy flows, where danger hides behind familiarity. You don't perform safely, you embody it. The safety mindset is not fear-based, but respect-based. Fear freezes; respect focuses. Fear says, "Be careful." Respect says, "Be present."

The Psychology of a Safety Mindset

Adopting this way of thinking requires rewiring how your brain processes routine and risk. You're not born cautious; you're trained through repetition and self-awareness. Fortunately, psychology gives us proven methods to change a mindset without breaking yourself psychologically.

Mindfulness Over Hypervigilance

The goal isn't to be paranoid, it's to be present. Mindfulness teaches us to observe without panic. Take a slow breath before activating a tool. Touch the switch deliberately. Visualize the path of motion before you begin. Every conscious pause reinforces the neural pathway of awareness.

Micro-Habits Replace Big Warnings

You don't need dramatic speeches to change behavior, just tiny, consistent cues. Hang your goggles in plain sight. Keep gloves beside the tool, not in a drawer. Say out loud, "Power off, tool down," before walking away. Small rituals build automatic responses that become identity-level habits.

Self-Compassion Over Self-Criticism

Awareness isn't weakness, it's mastery. When you forget something, don't spiral into guilt; note it, correct it, and practice differently next time. Learning is safer when mistakes lead to adjustment, not shame.

Maker's Mindset

Modeling Behavior Reinforces Identity.

Humans mirror what they see. If you treat safety as sacred, others will, too. Every act of awareness is a quiet form of leadership.

Learning the Hard Way

Some people learn by reading. Others by watching. I learned through pain. As a teenager, I crawled under an old '62 Ford Falcon, wrong wrench, wrong bolts, greasy hands. The wrench slipped; my knuckles met with steel. Later, I overloaded a hoist because I thought I could handle "just a bit more weight." It collapsed on my shin. The scar faded, but the lesson remained. I was lucky. But "lucky" isn't a safety plan.

Experience only teaches when it doesn't cost you a limb. The better teacher reflects on the habit of asking before how. True safety isn't learned through pain. It's learned through awareness before regret.

The Quiet Discipline of Awareness

Before a tool is touched, I hold a safety brief, not to lecture, but to reset attention. When we pause to review where our eyes, hands, and minds need to be, we rewire the brain's automatic pilot into conscious motion. After a few months, students stop waiting for the briefing. They anticipate it. They think it. They live it. That's when I know the mindset has taken root.

Safety isn't about memorizing the rules; it's about making awareness reflexive. When you reach that point, safety isn't something you remember to do, it's something you can't forget to be.

Reframing Responsibility

Every year, more than a thousand construction workers in the U.S. lose their lives, nearly all in preventable incidents. Not every story makes the news, but every one of those fatal mishaps leaves an empty chair at the dinner table. Safety begins with you. But it doesn't end with you.

When you practice awareness, you protect others. When you model it, you normalize it. When you speak up, you save someone else from silence. Every time you choose patience over hurry, precision over impulse, respect over pride, you strengthen the culture that keeps us all alive.

Becoming the Mindset

Safety is not the thing you do before you create.
It's the way you exist while you create. It's not an extra step; it's the thread running through every step. It's a quiet conversation between mind and body, between thought and motion. When you live in that awareness, every movement becomes deliberate, every decision ethically, every project sustainable.

The truly safe maker isn't careful because they fear consequences, they're careful because they respect creation. Safety is not a pause before life, it is life, practiced with reverence.

That's why it's Rule Zero.

Because before you do anything else, you must make yourself aware.

Maker's Mindset

Adopting the Safety Mindset (Practical Guide)

Start Each Day with Awareness. Before you touch a tool, stop and take a full, conscious breath. Ask:

What am I about to do?

What could this tool do if I lose focus?

Use "Reset Moments."

Between tasks, perform a mini mental check: posture, placement, path, people.

Keep a "Safety Journal."

After projects, note where you felt rushed, distracted, or unaware. Reflection trains pattern recognition.

Replace Fear with Curiosity.

When something feels risky, ask why it feels that way. Curiosity transforms fear into insight.

Celebrate Awareness, Not Luck.

Don't praise "nothing went wrong." Praise the times you prevented it from going wrong through patience and awareness.

Pair with a "Safety Buddy."

Partner with someone who keeps you accountable, not as a supervisor but as a mirror.

Close the Day with Gratitude.

The final step of any build: say thank you, to your tools, your hands, your awareness. Gratitude reinforces respect, and respect sustains mindfulness. "Safety isn't about slowing down; it's about staying around."

As described earlier, the Maker's Mindset is a system. Safety is the condition that allows every other rule to function at all.

How to Adopt This Mindset

Start with Humor, End with Reflection. Open with a laugh; close with a truth. Let humor set the hook, and reflection sink it in.

Model the Language

When you catch yourself making a near-miss mistake, own it out loud: "Well, that was stupid."
Students see that humility is strength, not weakness.

Celebrate Correction, Not Perfection

Praise the kid who catches an unsafe act, not the one who hides it. Safety is everyone's scoreboard.

Keep Consequences Visible

Discuss near misses openly. Frame them as "experience credits" rather than punishments.

Repeat the Mantra

Every time a tool hums or a machine starts, ask:
"What's the stupid thing we're not going to do today?"
The laughter that follows keeps awareness alive.

How It Reinforces the Safety Mindset

Reflection before reaction: Students pause before acting.

Ownership of choice: Responsibility shifts inward.

Maker's Mindset

Humor as memory: The lesson sticks because it's joyful.

Connection over correction: The teacher becomes a mentor, not a warden. When humor and awareness coexist, students learn to think with you, not just obey you. "If laughter saves a finger, then humor is a safety device." Every laugh shared over a "stupid" choice is one less real injury later. That's not just clever teaching, that's emotional engineering. We're wiring safety into the human experience.

The Psychology of Humor and Learning

Laughter releases endorphins and lowers cortisol. It keeps the brain from going into defense mode. In that relaxed state, students retain what you teach. Psychologists call this cognitive anchoring. When humor and learning occur together, the brain fuses them into a single, lasting memory. So, when a student later faces a risky decision, that same sense of humor replays in their head, a mental guardrail saying, "Don't play with stupid." It's not guilt. It's recall. That's the power of *Stupid Conversation*.

Turning Shame into Strength

The real secret is that I'm teaching emotional resilience, not just safety. In most environments, people are afraid to admit when they've made a mistake. They hide it, minimize it, or make light of the mistake. Here, the joke is the lesson. By laughing together at "stupid," we take away its sting. It stops being a label and becomes a learning moment. The fear of embarrassment is replaced by a shared language of honesty. Students start to see mistakes not as personal failure, but as feedback. And once that happens, safety consequences stop being about punishment, it becomes about partnership.

Why It Matters Beyond the Classroom

When I hear a student use "stupid" correctly, meaning reckless choice, preventable error, unnecessary risk, I know they've internalized the deeper rule: Safety is awareness in action.

In the real world, most accidents happen not because people don't know the rules, but because they forget to stay aware. They get comfortable. They rush. They assume nothing will go wrong. The stupid conversation teaches humility. It reminds us that no one, not even the expert, is immune to a lapse of attention. That humility saves lives.

Maker's Mindset

Deep Dive 0.1: The Stupid Conversation

Core Purpose: To show that safety is a mindset born from awareness, reflection, and humor, not from fear.

Humor creates connection; connection creates memory; memory creates safer habits.

The Story

Every semester, I start with what I call "The Stupid Conversation". Not because I think students are stupid, but because I need them to understand what stupid really means.

I'll call a kid over, usually the one who's already smirking, already curious.

"Hey, Goofy Kid, yeah, you. Come here. Have we had

The Stupid Conversation yet?"

They shake their heads or stare at me with curious but cautious expressions, unsure where this is going.

Stupid is an action, a verb, a choice, something that you do. Never a person, so let's review.

Me: "Running with scissors?"

Kid(s): "Stupid."

Me: "Sticking a fork in a wall outlet?"

Kid(s): "Super stupid."

Me: "Cussing in front of the principal's office?"

Kid(s): "Extra stupid!"

Then I lean in and say, "And what does stupid have?" They answer together, half-laughing, half-nervous, "Consequences."

Me: "Great, I will see you in detention with a safety brief."

They laugh because it's funny, but they remember because it's true. Humor disarms their defensiveness. Laughter opens the door to learning.

When the Lesson Sticks

A few weeks later, during a soldering lab, that same student shouted across the room,

"Hey, don't play with stupid, that iron's hot!" He said it instinctively. Not out of mockery, but out of care. I didn't need to say a word. Culture was doing its job. That's the goal, turning awareness into reflexes, and reflex into protection. Once that happens, "stupid" becomes less of an insult and more of a safety system or a playful way of saying, "I care enough to stop you before you get hurt."

Deep Dive 0.2: PPE Is Non-Negotiable

Core Purpose: To demonstrate that Personal Protective Equipment (PPE) is not a checklist, it's the physical expression of awareness. Wearing protection isn't about fear. It's about respect: for life, for tools, and for each other.

The Principle

Let me be clear. PPE is non-negotiable. It isn't a suggestion or red taps, it's your first and last line of defense. If you skip it, you're not saving time, you're gambling with your hands, your sight, and your future.

I've heard it a hundred times:

"It's just one quick cut."

"The safety glasses fog up."

"I'll only be at the grinder for a second."

And then I hold up a ruined glove, a pitted lens, or a scorched sleeve and ask, "How fast does an accident happen?" Every class has one student who learns that lesson the hard way. One year, a quiet eighth-grader refused gloves during a hot-glue build, just a second, she said. That second became a blister that lasted a week. The next day, she was the loudest PPE advocate in the room. Awareness teaches well. Pain is a harsh and unforgiving teacher.

Why It Matters

In a maker's world you'll face heat, sparks, edges, solvents, and the unpredictable. Creativity demands courage, but not recklessness. There's a razor-thin line between exploration and endangerment; PPE keeps that line visible.

For teachers and mentors, the stakes multiply.
Students mirror what you model. If you skip the goggles, they will too.
Neuroscience calls this mirror-neuron learning: people copy what they see,
not what they hear. If I model lazy safety, I'm silently giving permission for
injury. So, every time I pull on gloves or tighten my face shield, I'm
teaching something deeper: *Discipline over ego. Respect over convenience.*
Awareness over speed.

The Philosophy of Gear

Every piece of PPE protects more than flesh, it protects function.
Goggles guard curiosity; they let you keep seeing the world you're trying to
improve. Gloves guard craftsmanship; they protect the hands that turn
imagination into matter. Masks guard connection; they protect the
conversations you'll still have tomorrow.

Aprons, sleeves, and shields guard experience; they preserve the
lessons you've yet to learn.

When you gear up, you're not prepared for danger, you're
preparing for longevity. You're saying, "I respect my future self-enough to
stay whole."

A Story of Pride

During a visit to a community college fabrication lab where every
student had personalized their PPE. Stickers, initials, bright tape stripes, it
looked chaotic until you realized what it meant: ownership. They weren't
forced to wear gear; they wanted to. A student told me, "These gloves are

my tools, too." That statement stuck. PPE becomes a badge of professionalism when people take pride in it.

In my classroom, we now mark goggles with names. The rule is simple: No name, no use. If you name it, you'll protect it, and by extension, yourself.

Mindset Reinforcement

Respect through ritual; Every time you gear up, you rehearse awareness. Identity signaling: The act of wearing PPE says, I belong to a culture that values safety.

Teaching by example: Students copy what they witness, not what they're told. Discipline over ego: No one is "too cool" to be careful.[3]

When everyone gears up together, it's not compliance, it's choreography. The sound of gloves snapping and goggles tightening is the music of mindfulness.

Practical Integration

Design for Visibility. Store PPE in the open. Gear hidden in a drawer becomes gear forgotten.

Gear-Check Drill. Start every build with a quick call-and-response:

"Eyes?" – "Covered!"

"Hands?" – "Protected!"

"Mind?" – "Focused!"

---

[3] I see a lot of people on bikes and scooters not wearing PPE because it's not cool.

First Line of Respect Station. Label PPE shelves with that phrase; make it part of the culture's language. Accessible Options. Keep wipes, extra gloves, and multiple goggle sizes. Discomfort is the enemy of compliance, comfort removes excuses.

Reflection Wall.

After each project, post a 3×5 card answering, "What gear saved me today?"

The Psychological Anchor

Every time you reach for PPE, your brain forms a transition cue: "Now I'm entering a state of focus."
It's a form of embodied mindfulness, body leading mind. Over time, this ritual rewires the habit loop: the brain learns that safety gear = readiness. That's why seasoned makers seem calm even in complex environments, they've trained that calm through repetition.

Behavioral scientists call this anchoring through physical ritual. You can't teach awareness with a lecture, but you can trigger it with a habit. PPE is that trigger.

The Culture of Respect

When you see someone working without gear, speak up, not as a cop, but as a colleague. A simple "Gloves, please," said with respect, protects more than the hands, it protects the community. Safety enforced through fear creates silence. Safety reinforced through respect creates accountability.

Maker's Mindset

That's how we build the kind of shop where awareness becomes instinct and pride replaces excuses.

Maker's Moment

"Wearing PPE isn't compliancy; it's gratitude in motion." Each glove pulled tight is a thank-you to tomorrow.

Each lens cleaned is an act of respect for your own vision and every time you model that, someone else learns what real professionalism looks like.

Deep Dive 0.3: Experience Is the Better Teacher

Core Purpose: To show that while experience can be a powerful teacher, it doesn't have to come at the cost of pain. True wisdom lies in reflection, learning before the mistake happens, not after. Experience is only the best teacher if you survive it with awareness intact.

The Story

It's often said, "Experience is the best teacher." I used to agree with that, until I realized how expensive experience can be. Years ago, I watched a student learn the hard way. He was sanding a project, rushing to finish before the bell. The sander caught the edge, jerked his hand, and the board snapped in half.

He wasn't hurt, but the shock on his face told me everything. His project, three days of effort, was ruined in three seconds. He didn't need a lecture. He stood there, staring, breathing fast, and whispered, *"I should've slowed down."* That's when realization strikes: the lesson didn't come from the mistake itself, but from his reflection after. If he'd simply broken the board and walked away angry, he would've learned nothing. But he paused. He thought. He processed.

That's what makes experience a better teacher, not the pain, but the pause that follows.

The Myth of the Painful Lesson

People romanticize "hard lessons" like they're badges of honor. We say things like, "Well, I won't do that again!" and laugh it off, as if scars are proof of wisdom. But the truth is, most of those scars come from ignoring small signs. Experience can teach, yes, but pain is the most wasteful classroom there is. It takes time to heal, confidence to rebuild, and often money to replace what was lost. The real mastery comes from learning without bleeding. Every generation should inherit fewer scars than the last. That's how civilization and safety evolve.

Experience vs. Reflection

Experience without reflection is just repetition. You'll keep making the same mistake until you stop analyzing it. That's where the Safety Mindset steps in. it's not about doing more safely, it's about thinking more deeply. After any mishap, whether it's a tool jam, a burnt wire, or a project that fails to function, I ask students three questions:

1. What happened?
2. Why did it happen?
3. What could we do differently next time?

Simple questions, but profound results. Within minutes, their frustration transforms into understanding. Reflection turns the accident into a teacher rather than a punishment. That's the real feedback loop:

Observe. Reflect. Refine. Repeat.

Its engineering logic applied to life.

A Lesson from the Field

I once met a retired machinist with 40 years in the trade. His hands were a map of every cut, burn, and scar he'd ever earned. I asked him which scar taught him the most. He laughed and pointed not to his hands, but to a faded glove hanging on the wall, a scorched and melted at the fingertips. "That glove cost me one second of pride," he said, "and two weeks of healing. I keep it there so my apprentices don't need to make the same payment." He'd learned what I try to teach every student: You don't need to bleed to learn, you need to listen to those who did.

That's vicarious experience: wisdom passed down through storytelling and reflection. Every scar has a story, but the goal is not to collect stories, it's to prevent repeats.

Reflection Over Reaction

The difference between reactionary learning and reflective learning is emotional control. When something goes wrong, adrenaline floods your brain. It narrows focus and heightens emotion, good for survival, terrible for learning. If you immediately react ("That tool's junk!" or "I'll never try that again!"), you've closed the door on the lesson. But when you reflect, you reopen it. That's why I train students to pause before repairing or restarting after a mistake. We take one deep breath, sometimes two. We ask: "What just happened?" That breath resets the nervous system, turning panic into presence. Neuroscience calls this metacognition, thinking about your thinking. It's one of the highest forms of learning, and it's free if you make it a habit.

Maker's Mindset

Lessons Without Blood

In my classroom, I keep a bulletin board titled "Lessons Without Blood." Students can post quick reflections on near-misses, smart saves, or lessons learned from others. They write things like:

- *"Don't hold a 3D print too soon after the bed cools."*

- *"Keep long sleeves rolled up around the drill press."*

- *"Hot glue burns slower than it cools."*

It's not punishment, it's collective wisdom. Those reflections become the living textbook of the class.

What amazes me most is how proud they are of it. They take ownership of their awareness. And when new students join mid-semester, that wall teaches them more than any safety video ever could.

The Psychology of Safe Experience

The human brain learns through two main channels: experience and empathy. Experience builds neural pathways through direct feedback, touch, sound, sight, even pain. Empathy builds them through imagination and observation, seeing someone else's outcome and internalizing it. That's why storytelling, discussion, and debriefs matter. When we share our mistakes safely, others can learn without risk. This shared awareness forms what psychologists call a collective safety consciousness. Everyone's experience feeds into the same pool of learning. That's why reflection belongs to the group, not the individual. When one student pauses to reflect, twenty more learn vicariously.

Mindset Reinforcement

Awareness before arrogance: The best makers aren't fearless; they're mindful.

Reflection over repetition: A repeated mistake is a wasted experience.

Safe experience counts: You don't have to bleed to learn.

Shared learning saves lives: Your reflection might be someone else's prevention.

When you treat experience as data, not drama, the lesson stays and the pain fades.

Practical Integration

These are some of the best practices developed over a lifetime of learning:

1. **Post-Project Reflection Journals**: End every build day with two minutes of silent reflection. Ask: *What worked? What went wrong? What surprised me?*

2. **Incident Circles:** After a close call, gather the group. Speak without blame, share insights, and let peers offer observations.

3. **Legacy Lessons:** Keep visual reminders of old mistakes, cracked prints, bent screws, melted wire, displayed as humble teachers.

4. **The "Two-Minute Pause" Rule:** Before restarting after a failure, take two full minutes to review what happened. The delay saves time later.

Maker's Mindset

5. **Peer Reflection Cards:** Have team members or students document one thing they noticed someone else doing safely each week. It trains eyes, not just hands and adjusts mindsets.

Maker's Moment

"Wisdom doesn't need a scar. It just needs attention." Experience is only a great teacher when we listen to it. Reflection is how we keep its lessons without inheriting its wounds. When we pause long enough to learn safely, we honor every teacher who ever learned the hard way.

Safety is not the opposite of creativity. It is the foundation that makes creativity possible. When people feel protected, they take risks. When they trust the environment, they experiment. True innovation doesn't happen in fear-filled spaces; it happens where mistakes are survivable and learning is continuous. Safety is what gives makers permission to try, fail, and try again without hesitation.

Deep Dive 0.4: ALLSTOP & Safety Callout

Core Purpose: To establish a culture where every person, student, teacher, or teammate, shares responsibility for safety. This deep dive builds on *Stephen Covey's 8th Habit: "Find Your Voice."* In this classroom, "finding your voice" means speaking up without fear when something looks wrong, sounds wrong, or feels unsafe. Safety is not just my job, it's our job. In my classroom, with 20 or more students in motion, I can't be everywhere at once. There are always gaps in supervision, just like there are blind spots in the real world. That's why it's everyone's duty to be my eyes, my ears, and my awareness.

"**ALLSTOP**" is not a suggestion; it's a command. When someone shouts it, every person, every machine, and every movement halts immediately, no questions, no hesitation, no shame. Why? Because prevention happens in the seconds before an accident, not after. The ALLSTOP rule protects against the unseen and the unexpected:

Tools that cut or burn.

Objects that fly or fling

Materials that puncture, score, or snap

Any moment when proper awareness was not engaged. AllSTOP only works when everyone believes their voice matters. This isn't about authority; it's about shared humanity.

The "***Find Your Voice***" Connection Stephen Covey wrote that the 8th Habit is to "Find your voice and inspire others to find theirs." In a maker's space, that voice might prevent tragedy. Empowerment means replacing fear of embarrassment with pride in awareness. When a student calls "ALLSTOP," they are not tattling or disrupting, they are protecting their community. And when others respond without hesitation, that's trust. That's teamwork.

Building the ALLSTOP Culture

Teach It Early and Practice Often. Introduce the ALLSTOP rule on day one. Rehearse it as a group until it becomes instinct.

Normalize the Pause. Randomly call "ALLSTOP" during a build or lab then review what everyone did right. The pause becomes a drill for calmness, not chaos. Empower Everyone. Visitors, paraprofessionals, even first-day students, everyone gets the same authority. If you see danger, you own that voice.

Honor the Caller. When someone calls ALLSTOP, respond with gratitude, not irritation. They just protected someone you care about.

Reflect and Reset. After each ALLSTOP, discuss what triggered it and what can be improved. This turns awareness into wisdom.

Why It Matters. Every accident prevented begins as a moment noticed by someone alert. You can't automate that. You can't supervise it into existence. You have to teach courage needed to interrupt the flow for the right reason.

This is how we build responsible makers, strong teams, and confident leaders. The ALLSTOP mindset teaches that awareness and action belong to everyone.

Maker's Moment

"True leadership begins when someone has the courage to say, 'Stop.'" ALLSTOP isn't about fear, it's about care. When everyone finds their voice, safety becomes a shared heartbeat.

Final Note, The Enemy of Safety

The greatest enemy of safety is *complacency*, The quiet assumption that "nothing will happen." It is the moment when familiarity dulls awareness, when routine replaces reflection, and when confidence overshadows caution. Complacency, disregard for rules and protocols, and poor attention to environment and detail cause most mishaps. Every accident, every "close call," every burn or cut or spill has a cause, and most causes are preventable. Some hazards are obvious and predictable. Others appear suddenly and without warning. But even the unpredictable can be met with resilience when individuals and teams operate with the "Safety Is Paramount" mindset. This mindset is not a slogan. It's a living discipline. It means watching your surroundings, honoring the process, and trusting each other enough to speak up. It means preparing before acting, checking before assuming, and reflecting after every task.

Complacency is the enemy of safety, and it is that enemy that convinces people they no longer need the system.

Safety is not what you wear. It's what you think. It's the invisible awareness that binds every person, tool, and motion into one coordinated act of care. So, whether you are building, coding, welding, or teaching, stay aware, stay humble, stay vigilant.

This page was redacted and deleted by some secret government agency.

Most likely the Federal Meter Maid Service.

IT HAS TO WORK BEFORE IT LOOKS GOOD.

Mindset Rule One

Function Before Fashion

Every year, when I introduce a new design project, whether 3D modeling, robotics, or prototyping, there's a predictable pattern. Before the first sketch is functional, before the first print has even cooled, I see it: glitter, paint, logos, colors, stickers. Students rush to make their creations look finished before they've proven they work.

And I get it. That impulse is human. We're wired to value beauty. Our brains make split-second judgments based on appearance; it's part of our survival instinct. We read faces, shapes, and colors in milliseconds. In design, this translates into a deep psychological bias called the aesthetic-usability effect: the tendency to believe that beautiful things work better.

But here's the problem, beautiful lies are still lies. When something looks finished, our brains reward us with dopamine, the chemical of satisfaction. We feel like we've accomplished something. The project looks polished, so it must be good, right? Yet in truth, we've built an illusion.

Why "Pretty First" Thinking Hurts Designers
This is why I talk at length about function during the design phase. The hardest lesson for students, and often for adults, is that beauty cannot save

a design that doesn't work. A bridge painted gold will still collapse if its math is wrong. A product with sleek curves is worthless if it fails its purpose.

Students want to skip straight to the part that feels rewarding. And modern technology makes it easier than ever to do so. With 3D printers, laser cutters, and instant modeling software, they can produce something that looks market-ready in hours. It's fast, it's shiny, and it's empty.

That's why I publicly state that I hope their first iteration fails the functionality test. Not out of cynicism, but because failure forces honesty.

When a print doesn't fit, when gears bind, when something breaks under pressure, those are moments of clarity. Function exposes truth. It shows what really works and what's still imagination. Aesthetic perfection hides that truth behind false confidence.

As I tell my students: "Make it work before you make it pretty."

The Psychology Behind the Trap

The designer's brain is a strange machine. We crave closure. We love the feeling of finishing something. That "done" moment triggers the same neural reward as solving a puzzle or winning a game. The faster we can reach it, the better we feel. But the maker's world runs on a different clock. Function doesn't care about dopamine. Function cares about discipline, feedback, and iteration.

When you build something that doesn't work, you're staring at a mirror of your own assumptions. It's uncomfortable, but it's growth. The maker mindset rewires the brain's reward system: from celebrating completion to celebrating correction.

Maker's Mindset

The first version exists to fail. The second exists to improve. The third begins to work. And by the time you reach the fourth, you're no longer guessing, you're designing. Iteration is not repair; it's evolution. That's what separates hobbyists from engineers.

Function as Truth

Every field of creation, design, architecture, engineering, starts with the same universal law: form follows function. A designer who prioritizes function first learns to think in systems, not surfaces. Every curve, every joint, every choice must serve a purpose.

Fashion becomes the echo of performance. An architect who embraces this mindset begins to see structure as poetry. A well-designed building isn't beautiful because it's ornate, it's beautiful because it stands, breathes, and flows naturally within its purpose. The columns, arches, and spans aren't decoration; they are the rhythm of integrity made visible.

A maker who works for function first develops empathy. They start thinking about who the design serves, how it will be used, and why it must last. That empathy breeds precision. Every screw, every solder joint, every print layer begins to carry intention. When function leads, fashion follows gracefully. When fashion leads, function fails silently.

Design Psychology and the Ego

The hardest part of teaching design isn't explaining CAD tools or material tolerances, it's teaching humility. Students often equate how a design looks with how they look. When a model fails, they feel like they've failed. That ego attachment blocks learning.

True design maturity happens the moment a student can tear apart something beautiful because it doesn't work. That's when they've separated self-worth from aesthetic worth. They're no longer artists painting the surface, they're engineers sculpting the unseen. That shift in thinking changes everything. It allows critique to become data instead of judgment. It turns mistakes into metrics. And it frees the designer from vanity, which is the enemy of progress.

Iteration as Intelligence

I often tell my students that failure is feedback disguised as noise. The first prototype isn't supposed to impress anyone; it's supposed to teach you something you didn't know.

Each iteration rewires intuition. The maker begins to feel what will fail before it does. That's real intelligence, the quiet understanding born from experience. Psychologists call this cognitive flexibility, the ability to adapt thinking based on new evidence.

In every discipline, from art to aerospace, cognitive flexibility is what defines mastery.

The function-first mindset cultivates that skill naturally. It teaches you to value questions over appearances.

Aesthetic thinkers chase applause. Functional thinkers chase insight. One stops when it looks good; the other keeps going until it is good.

The Maker's Correction

When I watch students tinker with 3D printers, I remind them:

Maker's Mindset

"Plastic is cheap, time is not."

Don't decorate failure, diagnose it. We run print after print, each one slightly closer to working. The first wobbles. The second binds. The third spins cleanly, ugly and uneven but functional. And when it finally works, I tell them: Now you can make it pretty.

That sequence of events, failure, correction, success, is the heartbeat of design. It's the same process used by professional engineers, architects, and industrial designers. It's how every innovation begins: ugly, raw, and imperfect.

A beautiful bridge is not drawn; it's discovered, in calculations, corrections, and constraints. A graceful product is not designed in Photoshop; it's refined in the workshop. True beauty is the by-product of precision.

From Fashion to Mastery

Moving into this mindset transforms students into thinkers rather than decorators. Designers trained in function learn to ask why before how. They create things that solve problems, not just please eyes. Their work endures because it serves. Architects who prioritize structure and purpose create spaces that breathe, buildings that feel right because they are right. Beauty becomes the harmony of engineering and art, not their competition.

Makers who embrace iteration become inventors. They see failure as data, not defeat. Their hands learn the logic of materials, and their designs evolve like living systems. In every field, the function-first mindset cultivates a quiet kind of genius, the ability to turn constraints into creativity.

From Classroom to Craft

When my students start a project now, they already know what's coming. They smile nervously when I say it: "I hope your first print fails." And when it does, we gather around it, not to criticize, but to learn. We talk about alignment, torque, balance, and tolerance. We test assumptions. The lesson lands not because I lectured, but because they felt the difference between a pretty failure and a functional success. It's a moment of transformation every teacher lives for, the spark when frustration becomes fascination.

When function wins, the maker wakes up.

Closing Reflection

Fashion will always tempt us. It's the shortcut to approval, the fast track to dopamine. But the function-first mindset demands patience, humility, and truth. Every professional who truly understands design, engineers, architects, artists, makers, arrives at the same revelation: "The most beautiful things in the world are beautiful because they work."

A bridge, a violin, a prosthetic hand, a spacecraft, each began as something ugly that worked, and through refinement, became something beautiful that endured. So don't fear the ugly prototype. Don't decorate your mistakes. Don't worship polish before proof. Because when you chase function first, fashion finds you naturally. And when it does, it won't just look right, it will be right.

Deep Dive 1.1, The Oak Grove Lesson

When I was a kid in Scouts, we were taken to a wide, empty field just beyond the edge of town. The ground was uneven and mostly bare, broken only by weeds and the occasional stubborn patch of grass. Our Scout leader stood there with a small box of acorns, each one barely the size of a thumb. He told us we were going to plant trees, oaks, to be exact.

We looked at him like he was crazy. It was summer. The ground was dry and hard, and none of us wanted to spend the day digging holes for something we'd never see grow. We were twelve, maybe thirteen years old. The idea of planting trees that wouldn't be tall enough to climb for decades seemed like a cruel joke.

One of us finally asked, "Why are we doing this? They won't even be big until we're old." Our leader smiled. "Because someone will need the shade." That was it. No lecture, no big speech. Just that one quiet truth. So, we planted. We dug small holes, dropped acorns, covered them gently, and moved on. A few of us joked about coming back in a hundred years to see if they were still there. It felt pointless. But it wasn't.

Twenty years later, I drove past that same field. The weeds were gone. In their place stood a small grove of oaks, straight, proud, and strong. I pulled over and just sat there for a moment, realizing I was looking at proof that time rewards patience. Those trees weren't planted for me, but they carried my fingerprints all the same.

I learned much later in life that this was a lesson often repeated to young teens throughout the ages.

Maker's Mindset

The Psychology of Vision

Most people don't plan for futures they'll never see. It's not because they don't care, it's because the human brain is wired for immediacy. We crave short-term results. The same dopamine hit that drives students to decorate their first prototype also drives adults to rush projects, chase trends, or expect instant results. But lasting design, real design, requires patience.

Patience is the cognitive ability to delay gratification for the sake of greater reward. It's also the spiritual discipline of trusting that your effort has value, even if the reward belongs to someone else. Psychologists call this time horizon thinking how far into the future a person can imagine the consequences of their actions. The wider your horizon, the more visionary your mindset becomes. Most children think in hours; adults think in weeks; but true designers, architects, and makers think in decades. They imagine futures where their work still serves, even when they're long gone.

When you expand your time horizon, you stop designing for now and start designing forever.

Patience as a Design Tool

Patience isn't passive, it's strategic. Architects use patience when they wait for materials to settle before loading a structure. Engineers apply patience when they test and retest designs under stress. Even artists show patience when they let the paint dry before adding the next layer.

In the classroom, I teach that patience is as valuable as precision.

The student who rushes to the end of the project often misses the moment to learn something truly transformative.

We use 3D printers, coding platforms, and robotics, all tools built for speed, but I remind them that just because technology can go faster doesn't mean the mind should. The oak tree doesn't grow faster because you stare at it. It grows because you've given it the right conditions.

The Maker's Parallel

Every design has a life beyond its maker. A chair is meant to hold others. A bridge is meant to carry strangers. A building is meant to protect generations who will never know the architect's name. The oak grove is a metaphor for legacy in creation. When you build something with patience, you're not just solving a problem, you're planting potential.

Makers who understand this become guardians of time. They think about maintenance, durability, and adaptability. They ask, what happens when I'm not here to fix it? That mindset separates the maker from the tinkerer, the designer from the decorator. One builds for the moment; the other builds for the future.

Designing Beyond Yourself

Every time I give a new project to my students, I ask them to imagine someone else using it a year from now. It could be a sibling, a neighbor, or even a future student they'll never meet. "Design for them," I tell them, "not for me." When they do, their thinking changes. They stop chasing aesthetics and start considering ergonomics, safety, and accessibility. They start to care about the why behind the what.

Maker's Mindset

That's when I know the oak grove lesson has taken root. Makers who think this way develop empathy. They understand that their work will exist in other people's hands, spaces, and lives. That awareness brings purpose to every design decision.

Patience and Purpose

There's a saying I love: *We plant trees not for ourselves, but for those who come after.* The first time I heard it, it sounded poetic. Now I realize it's the blueprint for sustainable design, leadership, and even teaching. Everything meaningful in life, education, architecture, craftsmanship, relationships, requires you to start something you may never finish.

That's not a flaw; that's faith. Faith that your contribution will matter. Faith that what you build will endure. When I think of that oak grove, I don't remember the heat, the dirt, or the impatience. I remember standing there as a kid, completely unaware that I was taking part in a generational design project. We planted more trees that day. We planted perspective.

The Long Game of Making

Designers who understand patience evolve differently. They don't panic when a prototype fails; they see it as an iteration. They don't chase perfection, they pursue endurance. Architects who think long-term build structures that adapt with the environment, not against it. Engineers who design with patience make technologies that are repairable and upgradable. Makers who value time create projects that remain useful even after trends fade.

The world has enough instant products. What it needs are enduring ones.

Reflection

As a teacher, I realize now that my role isn't to make students fast, it's to make them thoughtful. The maker who learns patience doesn't just finish a project; they start a legacy. The oak grove reminds me that the true reward of creation isn't recognition, it's contribution. Those oaks don't carry my name, but they carry my intention. They stand quietly, offering shade to people who don't know I was ever there. And that's the beauty of it.

Because that's what every great design, invention, or act of kindness really is, a seed planted for someone else's comfort.

"Legacy isn't built in the rush of creation; it's planted in patience." When I drive by that field now, the oaks are taller than I ever imagined. Their roots are deep, their canopies wide. I realize that design, like those trees, is an act of faith in the future, proof that good work takes time. And sometimes, the best thing a maker can do is start something knowing they'll never see it finished.

Maker's Mindset

Deep Dive 1.2, The Outdoor Shower

There are moments in every maker's life when an idea burns brighter than reason. For me, that spark first lit inside an old Plymouth station wagon.

The Plymouth Water Heater Experiment

When I was about eight, my brother and I decided that warm water was a right, not a luxury.

Armed with a garden hose, two cans of black spray paint, and the reckless confidence of youth, we looped the hose inside our non-running Plymouth. We figured if sunlight could heat a car to oven temperatures, it could surely heat water. So, from inside the car, we spray-painted the hose black for "better heat absorption." Science was sound enough for kids our age, safety, not so much.

It worked, beautifully, for about five minutes. The water ran hot, the air filled with chemical fumes, and for one shining moment, we believed we'd invented solar power.

…Then the hose burst. Steam, paint fumes, and chaos erupted in a single hiss of pressure. Our triumph turned instantly into our mother's fury. I don't think she's ever yelled louder, or faster, before or since.

The lesson stuck: sometimes, the only way to learn how things work is to watch them fail spectacularly.

The Adult Version , A Maker's Upgrade

Decades later, that memory resurfaced when I faced a similar problem: How do you rinse off after a day of yard work without freezing to death?

My home has two upstairs showers, none downstairs. Every time I came in covered in dirt or grass, I either tracked it through the house or endured the icy blast of a garden hose. The hose solution worked fine in August but was misery in early spring and late fall. So, I decided to build an outdoor shower, functional, warm, and simple. And much like the doghouse from my youth, I had visions far grander than practicality demanded: a ten-person solar-powered spa with a thirty-two-point massage jet, powered by what I jokingly called a fusion reactor, the sun. But before a single cut or fitting, I promised myself something new: I would plan it. So, I opened my "Vision and Plan" worksheet.

Project Vision

Title: Outdoor Shower with Warm Water

Purpose: Rinse off dirt, sweat, and dog hair without depleting household hot water.

Vision: Year-round, fully operable hot-and-cold shower near the future pool area.

Constraints:

1. No water, power, or gas lines in the northeast corner of the yard.

2. Must be safe, winterizable, and inexpensive.

Safety Concerns:

Hand-tool injuries, PVC fumes, and the occasional unexpected splash zone.

I drew out the design and brainstormed heating concepts, each one more creative (and occasionally ridiculous) than the last.

Option A , The Sand Heater

> **Idea:** Bury a coiled garden hose in sand and paint everything black to trap heat.

> **Result:** Worked for about 30 seconds. The sand never warmed enough to retain heat.

> **Lesson:** Heat transfer looks better on paper than it feels on bare feet.

Option B, The Glass Tank Heater

> **Idea:** Use a five-gallon glass bottle with copper tubing coiled inside.

> **Result:** Worked, for about a minute. The water flashed hot, then lost heat immediately.

> **Lesson:** Glass radiates heat faster than it stores it. Beautiful, but inefficient.

Option C, The Competition Heater

> **Idea:** Adapt the ten-quart boiling-pot system I'd once used at BBQ competitions with my father-in-law and good friend, Tom Ouellette.

> **Result:** Worked too well. The water hit near-industrial temperatures.

> Practical for ribs, not for people.

Option D, The Commercial Solar Bag

> **Idea:** Buy a ready-made solar shower, fill, hang, enjoy.

> **Result:** Worked, until the bag emptied mid-rinse. Hope you're

done soaping.

Lesson: Never trust gravity to manage your hygiene schedule.

From Vision to Reality

After days of research, sketching, and watching every solar-heated tutorial on YouTube, I committed to Option A.

I laid out 80 feet of Schedule-40 PVC, glued adapters, sealed joints, and built a heater core packed with play sand. Each piece fit together like a puzzle I'd cut myself.

For forty-eight hours, the structure cured under the Texas sun. When I finally turned on the tap, warm water poured out, steady, gentle, glorious. It wasn't pretty. It looked like a science-fair project had married a plumbing accident. But it worked, and that was enough.

The Psychology of Proof of Concept

What I had built was not a final product; it was a proof of concept. And that's the most powerful step in any maker's process. Proof of concept asks a simple, brutal question: Does it work in reality? Not does it look good, nor will it impress someone, but does it perform?

The human mind loves polish, we crave immediate success and smooth finishes, but true design happens in the messy middle. Psychologists call this the learning loop: test, fail, observe, adjust, repeat. Every iteration rewires understanding. That's what separates a builder from a tinkerer. The tinkerer celebrates the build; the builder celebrates the insight.

Maker's Mindset

The Value of Experience

The outdoor shower taught me that no amount of reading replaces firsthand discovery. I could have memorized every principle of thermodynamics and still missed the nuances of flow rate, heat retention, and real-world durability. Experience teaches through the senses, sight, touch, sound, and sometimes panic.
You feel what works. You remember what it doesn't.

That's why I encourage my students to test their designs early and often. If it leaks, buzzes, or burns out, they've just earned a lesson that no worksheet can teach. Failure isn't the opposite of success; it's the scaffolding beneath it. Each attempt gives you clearer eyes for the next. Experience doesn't just teach what to build, it teaches how to think when building.

Learning as Iteration

By the time my outdoor shower stood operational, I had tested five prototypes, refined countless joints, and rebuilt the heating core twice. But those failures weren't wasted hours; they were data.

Iteration is not repetition; it's evolution. Every redesign improves understanding, not just outcomes. That's the lesson I bring into every classroom: the courage to learn publicly, to fail visibly, and to iterate intelligently. Because the only bad experiment is the one you never try.

Reflection

For two years, that ugly-beautiful shower served faithfully, until one particularly cold March when even the Texas sun abandoned me.

During the pandemic lockdown of 2020, with too much time to tinker, I finally upgraded it with an on-demand propane water heater. But I still miss the old solar model. It represented something deeper than comfort; it represented curiosity and turned tangible. Each failure, each leak, each small victory reinforced what I now teach my students every day: You don't learn by avoiding mistakes. You learn by chasing them down, fixing them, and building again.

Maker's Moment

"Experience doesn't hand out trophies, it hands out blueprints for your next attempt." The outdoor shower wasn't my prettiest creation, but it remains one of my proudest, because it embodies the maker's truth: Progress is rarely clean, but it's always worth getting your hands dirty.

Maker's Mindset

Most parents worry when the children grow quiet. Mine worried when the lights suddenly dimmed.

Thomas Burbridge

A Childhood Memory

MINDSET RULE TWO
START WITH WHAT WORKS

Mindset Rule Two

Start With What Works

There is a temptation in every new project to begin with a blank slate, to reinvent, redesign, and outdo everything that came before. But the truth is, innovation almost never begins with nothing. Every great idea, every leap in design or discovery, started by standing on something that already worked.

Whether it was a stone tool, a transistor, or a set of classroom rules, progress is built on the foundations that came before. This is not limitation, it's efficiency. The maker's mind recognizes that improvement is not the enemy of originality; it's the path to it.

The "I Wonder" Mindset

At the heart of all invention is curiosity. It begins quietly, with a question that lingers long enough to become an experiment. *"I wonder what would happen if..."* That phrase has launched more discoveries than any textbook ever printed. In the maker's world, this is where learning begins: not with tools, not with instructions, but with wonder. Before there is a design, there is a hypothesis. Before there is a breakthrough, there is play. Children are natural scientists. They poke, prod, and dismantle the world to see what's inside. The trick for adults, and educators, is not to suppress that instinct, but to refine it.

Curiosity is the ignition source. It burns bright, but it must be directed. And to direct it effectively, a maker must learn to set aside something far more dangerous than inexperience: ego.

Surrendering Ego to Curiosity

The hardest part of starting with what works is admitting that someone else got there first. That's where ego steps in. It whispers, "You can do it better," but what it really means is, "Don't look at their work, you might feel small." Ego doesn't like being a student; it prefers the title of expert. But curiosity demands humility.

To start with what works, you must first surrender the need for ownership. You must ask, what can I learn from this? instead of, how do I make it mine?

How does Ego and Bias Sabotage Learning

1. **Confirmation Bias:** Seeing only what supports your assumptions. Makers who are sure their ideas will work stop noticing data that says otherwise. Curiosity invites contradiction; ego rejects it.

2. **Dunning–Kruger Effect**: The less we know, the more we believe we know. Beginners often skip steps or ignore foundational skills because "it looks easy." Humility keeps us grounded enough to master basics before we leap.

3. **Sunk-Cost Fallacy**: When we've spent time or money, quitting feels like failure. Ego says, "Keep going so the effort isn't wasted." Curiosity says, "Maybe this approach was wrong, let's adjust."

Maker's Mindset

Status Quo Bias: Comfort prefers the familiar, even when it doesn't work. Ego defends the old way. Curiosity wonders, "What if there's a better way?"

The Paradox of Expertise

Even experts aren't immune. Experience breeds confidence, but unchecked confidence breeds blindness. The most advanced engineers and teachers sometimes forget what it means to learn from scratch. To keep growing, master's must periodically unlearn. They must re-enter beginner mode, revisit their assumptions, and let curiosity interrogate their own success.

That's why historical innovators like Faraday, Curie, and Edison were relentless note-takers. They weren't protecting pride; they were protecting data. They value accuracy over ego. Every experiment, failed or successful, was a stepping-stone for the next generation.

Humility as a Technical Skill

In the workshop, humility isn't weakness, it's intelligence. It keeps the focus on function, not fame.

When my students defend a design that clearly doesn't work, I remind them: *"The circuit doesn't care who built it. It only cares if it closes."*

The moment ego steps aside, teamwork ignites. Students begin testing ideas instead of defending them. Collaboration replaces competition. The classroom transforms from a gallery of personal projects into a laboratory of shared learning.

How to Disarm Ego and Engage Curiosity

1. **Prototype Anonymously:** Evaluate the work, not the worker. Function speaks louder than authorship.

2. **Reward Improvement, Not Perfection**: Celebrate iteration, not outcome.

3. **Keep an Engineering Notebook**: Record observations without judgment.

4. **Ask Instead of Announce:** Replace "I think this will work" with "I wonder if this will work."

Each of these shifts rewires the learning process from proving to discovering.

The Six-Step Maker's Scientific Process

Once ego is quiet, the real method begins, a simplified version of the scientific method that guides all engineering projects:

1. **The "*I Wonder*" Phrase, Curiosity**: Ask a question born from genuine wonder. This defines your purpose.

2. **The Research Phase, Observation:** Study what already exists. Deconstruct examples. Read, watch, and listen. Borrow success before inventing failure.

3. **The Prediction Phase, Hypothesis:** Form a testable idea: I suspect that if I do X, Y will happen.

4. **The Prototype Phase, Experimentation:** Build something, anything, that tests the idea. Perfection is irrelevant; feedback is gold.

5. **The Reflection Phase – Analysis:** Ask what worked, what didn't, and why. Focus on cause, not blame.

6. **The Documentation Phase, Learning:** Record results so you (and others) can build on them later. What gets written gets remembered. This is not a checklist, it's a mindset. It shifts the goal from being right to learning fast. The faster you learn, the more refined your creations become.

Why This Mindset Matters

Starting with what works doesn't mean copying; it means respecting physics, patterns, and principles.

Nature, technology, and human ingenuity all operate by consistent rules. When you understand those rules, you can bend them.

Great inventors don't reject existing systems; they build scaffolds on top of them. A musician studies scales before composing symphonies. An architect studies load distribution before designing cathedrals. A student studies working circuits before designing their own robots. Every masterpiece begins with a borrowed truth.

Psychology of Beginnings

Why is this so hard to teach? Because the human brain craves novelty. We mistake originality for value. The brain learns fastest through association, connecting the new to the known. When students start from scratch without reference, they face a cognitive cliff. But when they analyze an existing model, the brain scaffolds new information efficiently. It's not cheating, it's cognitive engineering. This is why *"Start With What Works"* isn't just philosophy; it's neuroscience. It aligns with how humans are wired to learn.

Maker's Moment

Before you can improve the world, you have to understand it. Curiosity, not pride, is where that understanding begins. The ego seeks praise. Curiosity seeks truth. Only one of them ever improves the design.

Maker's Mindset

Deep Dive 2.1, The Solar Hot Dog Maker

Some ideas begin with blueprints. Others begin with childhood television. This one began with both, and a roll of tin foil. In the early 1980s, my brother and I watched a show called *That's Incredible! *, where inventors, daredevils, and the mildly insane showcased creations that defied logic. One episode featured a solar-powered oven that cooked food using nothing more than reflected sunlight. For two boys armed with summer boredom and an old Weber grill, it was less a curiosity and more a calling.

We decided that day to build our own solar-powered hot dog maker. Not a grill, not a stove, something revolutionary. Something our mother might even approve of. (She had banned us from cooking hamburgers after an earlier "smoke incident" involving a campfire and an unfortunate patch of lawn.)

Phase One: The Vision

Our grand design began with the materials we had: One rusted-out Weber grill, partially dented from past adventures. Several yards of tin foil (the shiny kind). A few leftover hot dogs from the family refrigerator. And, of course, a sketch drawn on lined notebook paper that made perfect sense to us and no sense to anyone else.

We imagined the foil acting as a mirror, reflecting the sunlight onto a small cast-iron plate inside the grill. The hot dogs would sit upon that plate, basking in the concentrated rays of solar glory until they sizzled. It was elegant in theory, brilliant in our minds, and possibly hazardous in practice.

Armed with scissors, tape, and the overconfidence of youth, we set to work. Each piece of tin foil was carefully smoothed, aligned, and bent into crude parabolic reflectors. It looked like a space-age disco ball on a bad day, but to us, it gleamed like science itself.

Phase Two: The Setup

Around that same time, our household became one of the first on the block to own a VCR, a marvel of technology that could record television. This, to our minds, meant we could reply *That's Incredible! * as many times as necessary to perfect our solar cooker's design. We rewound, paused, and studied the TV inventor's technique like engineers poring over classified blueprints. The man in the show had used mirrors, glass covers, and precise angles. We had tinfoil, tape, and whatever faith an eight-year-old can muster.

By the end of the second day, our solar cooker was "finished." The foil gleamed, the hot dogs were placed ceremoniously in position, and the sun, our fusion reactor, was blazing overhead. We stood back, hands on hips, waiting for the miracle of heat transfer to begin.

Phase Three: The Waiting Game

Here's where our youthful enthusiasm met the wall of scientific reality. For ten minutes, nothing happened. At twenty minutes, we repositioned the foil to "catch more rays." At thirty minutes, we became certain something was wrong with the sun.

After about forty-five minutes, I lost interest and wandered off to do something far more engaging, like staring at ants or digging a hole in the yard. My brother, however, remained. He was the patient one, the steady hand to my restless mind. Before heading inside, he covered the hot dogs with an upside-down pot lid to keep flies away. And that's when he accidentally completed the design, the reflective foil caught the sun, the lid trapped the heat, and a crude convection system formed. Thirty minutes later, he came inside grinning, holding a half-eaten hot dog.

"It worked," he said through a mouthful of proof. And indeed, it had. The world's first (and possibly last) backyard solar-powered hot dog cooker had succeeded.

Phase Four: Reflection and Lessons

It's easy, decades later, to laugh at the absurdity of it all, the foil, the patience, the burnt hot dog, but that small backyard experiment taught me one of the most valuable lessons in design thinking: *Curiosity leads to discovery, but patience reveals truth.*

Our success wasn't due to perfect planning or technical skill. It was the product of trial, error, and a willingness to let the experiment teach us what we didn't know. We started with what worked, the basic principle that sunlight produces heat, and built from there.

And like most childhood inventions, it didn't just test physics, it tested ego. I had given up before the results appeared. My brother's quiet persistence proved what curiosity combined with patience can do.

The Maker's Mindset in Action

In hindsight, that little solar cooker was a perfect example of the Maker's Mindset at work:

1. **We started with what worked**. We copied the idea from TV, observed the process, and applied it with the materials we had. No shame in imitation, only the joy of understanding.

2. **We experimented boldly.** There was no safety manual, no "how-to" guide, just imagination and sunlight. We didn't fear failure because we didn't know to fear it.

3. **We observed and adjusted.** My brother's pot-lid improvisation turned an inert setup into a functioning one, a genuine example of real-world iteration.

4. **We learned from experience.** We didn't just build a solar cooker, we learned about reflection, convection, and perseverance. (And maybe about sharing credit.)

That project marked the beginning of a lifelong fascination with taking ideas from concept to function. Even as adults, many makers forget this simple truth: You don't have to start from scratch. You can start from someone else's success and build something new on top of it.

The Psychological Takeaway

That backyard experiment represents more than childhood ingenuity, it's a microcosm of how creativity functions in every age.

Human innovation is iterative. Each generation refines the work of the last. Yet ego often tricks us into believing that starting from zero proves genius. In reality, the smartest builders begin by observing what already works.

Even in professional engineering and design, we see the same psychological patterns we showed as kids: impatience, overconfidence, and distraction. The difference between a child's mistake and an expert's oversight is usually just the size of the budget.

True makers learn to temper enthusiasm with observation. They let curiosity do the thinking and humility do the learning. When you start with what works, you aren't copying, you're calibrating.

A Teacher's Reflection

When I tell this story to my students, they laugh at the image of two kids burning hot dogs with tinfoil. Then I point to the real lesson: *"You already know more than you think you do. The trick is learning how to use what works before trying to invent what doesn't."* in the classroom, "start with what works" translates to reverse-engineering success. I often ask students to examine everyday objects, a pen, a power strip, or a 3D-printed hinge, and explain how it functions before designing their own. Once they understand how something works, they can meaningfully improve it. That's the essence of design literacy: seeing function clearly enough to imagine better.

Maker's Moment

"The best discoveries rarely come from inventing something new. They come from seeing the ordinary through extraordinary curiosity."

Our solar hot dog maker wasn't a revolution. It was a reflection, literally and figuratively, of two young minds daring to wonder. And sometimes, wonder is all it takes to turn sunlight into supper.

Maker's Mindset

Deep Dive 2.2, Experience Is the Best Teacher

There's a saying in every workshop, from the shipyard to the science lab: "You don't really know how something works until you break it."

It's crude, but true. No textbook or lecture can replace the depth of understanding earned through experience. A burnt resistor, a misaligned gear, a toppled structure, each one teaches more about design than a thousand perfect examples ever could. When we start with what works, we're not just copying success. We're building a foundation for experience to teach us what the manual can't.

The Lessons You Can't Teach from a Book

I've spent enough years in classrooms and garages to see a pattern: the students who learn the most are the ones willing to fail the fastest. They're not reckless, they're engaged. They move beyond reading instructions and start reading outcomes.

Every misstep is a conversation with reality. Every error is feedback, not failure. Experience compresses lessons into muscle memory and emotional memory, how something feels when it's right, and how it sounds when it's wrong. That's the kind of knowledge that sticks. In education, we call this experiential learning. In the real world, we just call it life.

Experience Changes Understanding

Early in my teaching career, I assigned a simple bridge-building project to a group of middle school students. The rules were straightforward: construct a bridge using popsicle sticks and wood glue that could hold at least five pounds. The class split into two camps. One group dove in immediately, cutting, gluing, and stacking sticks into wild, ambitious shapes. The other group started by researching bridge types, truss, arch, suspension, and built small test models to see what failed and what held.

When the final test day came, the results were predictable: the research group's bridges stood firm. The rapid-build group's bridges snapped gloriously under pressure. But what struck me wasn't who "won." It was what happened afterward.

The students whose bridges failed weren't defeated; they were curious. They crouched over the splintered remains, running fingers along broken glue joints and muttering things like, "So that's where the weight shifted" or "I should've used triangles." That's the moment every teacher lives for, the spark of experience turning into understanding. The data was literally in their hands.

The Psychology of Learning by Doing

From a cognitive perspective, experience activates more regions of the brain than observation alone. When students touch, build, hear, and correct mistakes, their brains create layered associations between motion, emotion, and logic. It's the difference between watching a dance and learning the steps.

This multi-sensory encoding is what makes lessons "stick." It explains why you never forget how to ride a bike or solder a wire once you've done it, your neurons wired themselves to the rhythm of the action.

Maker's Mindset

But there's a catch: experience doesn't teach automatically. It only teaches those who are paying attention. Reflection is the second half of the equation.

Without reflection, experience becomes repetition. With reflection, it becomes wisdom.

Bringing It Back to the Maker's Mindset

When we "start with what works," we give experience something to build on. We don't waste time reinventing the wheel; we learn how the wheel turns, why it's shaped that way, and how to make it better. That's what separates a tinkerer from a designer. A tinker experiment without learning. A designer experiments with intention.

In a classroom, this looks like a student who fails a circuit test, checks the polarity, adjusts the resistor value, and tries again, each iteration guided by data, not luck. That process transforms frustration into fluency.

How to Teach Through Experience

Here are some ways that I have used to teach lessons through experience:

1. **Encourage Safe Failure:** Set up challenges where failure is frequent but harmless, so students associate it with learning, not punishment.

2. **Make Reflection Visible:** Require students to log what went wrong, what worked, and why. Reflection is what turns "I messed up" into "I learned something."

3. **Praise Curiosity, Not Perfection:** When you celebrate questions over correct answers, you rewire the reward system toward growth instead of performance.

4. **Model the Process:** When a teacher admits, "I'm not sure, let's test it," it shows students that learning is a shared act, not a one-way transaction.

The Difference Between Knowledge and Understanding

Knowledge is the collection of facts you can recite. Understanding is what you can recreate without looking it up. The moment a student uses prior failure to predict future success, they've crossed the bridge from memorization to mastery. That's experience doing its work. You can tell when it happens, the quiet grin after a motor spins, the soft "oh" when a beam finally balances, the proud shout when the code finally runs. That's learning at its most honest.

The Teacher's Paradox

Ironically, the more experience a teacher has, the harder it can be to let students learn this way. We've seen the mistakes before. We know where it's going wrong. Every instinct scream to intervene, to save time, save materials, save frustration. But in saving those things, we sometimes rob students of the very lessons that matter most. A maker learns through engagement, not efficiency. Sometimes the best way to teach is to step back and let the project talk.

Reflection: Experience and Ego

Experience, much like curiosity, demands humility. The more you think you know, the less you're willing to test. The moment you assume you're past failure is the moment you stop learning. I often tell students: "If you're not breaking things, you're not learning. Just make sure you break the right things first." Experience isn't about perfection, it's about progress. It's about learning how the world responds when you interact with it. It's about noticing patterns that others miss because they only read about them.

"The fastest way to learn is to do. The second fastest way is to fail and pay attention." Experience remains the only teacher that doesn't accept excuses. It hands out lessons whether you're ready or not, and the test always comes before the lecture. That's what makes it unforgettable, and why every maker, teacher, and learner should honor it as the truest path to understanding.

MINDSET RULE THREE
USE YOUR TOOLS

Mindset Rule Three

Use Your Tools

Take care of your tools and your tools will take care of you. That phrase has been shouted, whispered, and embroidered on every workshop apron since the Industrial Revolution.

I can still picture my cigarette-smoking uncle waving a wrench in one hand and his finger in the other, preaching that same line to a kid who only half understood its full meaning. Back then it sounded like grown-up noise.

Now, after a few decades of teaching, fixing, and building, I realize he was right, but not for the reasons he thought. Using your tools isn't just about screwdrivers, hammers, and other objects for the hands. It's about using everything available to you, your hands, your mind, your heart, and your community, to build something that works.

The tool might be a soldering iron, a spreadsheet, or a kind word spoken at the right moment.

All of them matter. All of them require care.

A tool for the Hand

Physical tools are the easiest to see and the hardest to respect. They live in drawers, boxes, and benches until we forget where we left them. Then, at the worst possible moment, the socket's missing, the blade's dull, or the battery's dead.

A cared-for tool doesn't wander off.

Tools left in the rain rust. Sharp tools stored carelessly draw blood. A wrench used as a hammer will snap when it matters most. Every dent and chip tells a story of neglect or respect. My father once told me, "Things are worth more when you have to pay to replace them." I didn't get it until I broke my first torque wrench and had to buy a new one with my own paycheck. Suddenly the idea of *take care of your tools* became very real.

In every workshop there's an invisible contract between maker and tool: Treat me right, and I'll make you look brilliant. Ignore me, and I'll betray you in front of the whole world.

Tools for the Mind

Not every tool fit in a toolbox. Some live behind your eyes. Your mind is the most powerful tool you own. It can create, connect, reason, and imagine, but it can also corrode. Bias is rust for the intellect; fear is sand in the gears. Astrophysicist **Dr. Neil deGrasse Tyson** once said our greatest tool is independent thought, the courage to question authority and separate belief from evidence. That's why I tell my students: the mind is both your workbench and your workshop.

We all carry biases, age, gender, culture, language, education. Pretending we don't only let them grow in the dark. Recognizing bias is like sharpening a blade; it keeps your thoughts clean and your curiosity honest.

Maker's Mindset

I've been guilty myself. Once at the gym I caught myself judging a guy in a tank top and bandanna who played basketball like he owned the court. I assumed attitude, not skill. Turns out he was a city engineer, the guy who literally keeps our traffic lights working. That moment smacked me harder than any rebound. My bias was showing, and it dulled my understanding of someone who could teach me something. An open mind doesn't mean believing everything; it means being willing to test everything.

That's the maker's way: question, test, observe, improve. If an idea breaks under evidence, good, it just saves you from building failure into your design. Mental tools need maintenance too. Sleep, curiosity, humility, and learning are their oil and polish.

When you stop feeding your brain new input, it locks up. A frozen mind can't innovate any more than a seized bearing can spin. So, keep your thinking tools sharp:

1. Read something outside your comfort zone.
2. Listen to someone who disagrees with you.
3. Take apart your own opinions and see what still fits.

The more perspectives you test, the more precise your understanding becomes.

Tools for the Heart (and the Community)

Here's where the metaphor gets real. People are tools too, but not in the slang sense. They're the most valuable, unpredictable, irreplaceable tools you'll ever work with. Treat them well, and they'll multiply your reach. Treat them poorly, and the whole machine grinds to a halt. I learned this early in both the Navy and the classroom. A well-maintained team performs like a well-oiled gear train: each tooth meshes, each motion builds on the next. But the moment one member feels disposable, the system fails.

No one is disposable.

Say it again.

No one.

A leader who treats people like single-use utensils may see short-term results, but they'll pay with human capital and eventually burn out. A classroom or workplace that values people only for output will never see innovation. Creativity doesn't grow under fear or contempt.

Your community is a toolbox. Every person adds something different, experience, perspective, patience, humor. Some are torque wrenches, some are feather dusters, and some are duct tape. When you learn to value every one of them, you build resilience into the system.

The Box You Build Together

We'll explore the "box of chalk vs. box of crayons" idea deeply in a later section, but it belongs here in spirit. A uniform team might look efficient, but a diverse one is efficient, because diversity brings adaptability. Different backgrounds, different ideas, different failures, they're all tools that strengthen the collective build. When you look into another person's toolbox, you might find the exact skill you didn't know you needed. **The heart of this mindset is acceptance.** Acceptance doesn't mean agreement; it means openness. When we accept the people, we work with, regardless of origin, status, or style, we expand what's possible. The more tools we bring to the table, the stronger the bridge we can build.

Fear: The Tool That Doesn't Belong

Of all the tools we carry, fear is the one that deserves to be locked away. Fear shuts down creativity faster than a power outage. As an educator, I've learned that fear and learning cannot share the same space. When a student is afraid of failing, of being wrong, of getting in trouble, learning stops.

When a teacher teaches in fear, of parents, admin, or politics, innovation stops. Once I was called into the principal's office over a social-media lesson titled "How a Lie Becomes the Perception of Truth." I walked down that hallway with my stomach twisting, imagining every worst-case scenario.

Fear brought its cousin, anger, along for the ride. Then I realized I was falling into the same trap I warn my students about[4]: reacting instead of reasoning. So, I reframed it as a design challenge. If communication had failed, how could I redesign it? By the end of that meeting, we weren't fighting, we were troubleshooting.

That's what happens when you take fear out of the toolbox. **Curiosity walks back in.** When I tell students, "Fear is optional. Curiosity is

---

[4] As an educator, it completely disgusts me how some people feel that teachers must be so perfect, that we create oceans of water before we prove our sainthood by walking on it. We *are* human and do human things outside of school.

required," I'm really talking about trust. Trust in themselves, trust in the process, and trust that even mistakes can become tools for learning.

Modern Tools, Ancient Wisdom

We live in a time when our tools learn back. Artificial intelligence, automation, digital fabrication, these are not replacements for creativity; they are amplifiers. AI, in particular, is like giving humanity a mirror-polished wrench: it can tighten brilliance or strip the threads of integrity, depending on the hands that use it. Some people fear AI will replace them. It won't, unless they refuse to learn how to use it. Just like any new tool, it demands respect, understanding, and ethical care.

A hammer can build a home or break a window; intent makes the difference. When I couldn't find reliable illustrators or editors for this book, AI became a temporary assistant, a way to translate vision into visual. It didn't replace human artistry; it helped bridge the gap between idea and creation. That's the essence of this rule: use your tools wisely, ethically, creatively.

Don't worship them, don't fear them, and don't ignore them. The mind that built the hammer built the computer. The heart that sought connection built the network. The same responsibility applies to taking care of your tools, and they'll take care of you.

The Psychology of Working in Teams (Why One Pair of Hands Is Never Enough)

No serious building happens alone for long. Even the myth of the lone genius falls apart under inspection. Behind every breakthrough is a quiet network of testers, critics, mentors, rivals, and helpers. Teams aren't just convenient; they're neurological force multipliers. Cognitive psychology tells us something makers have known forever: the brain is not designed to solve complex problems in isolation. Working memory is limited. Attention is fragile. When we collaborate, we offload mental load the same way we offload torque with a breaker bar. One person holds the frame. Another tightens the bolt. A third notices the alignment is off before anything snaps. Good teams distribute thinking the way good tools distribute force. In healthy groups, individuals don't just add effort, they add difference. One person spots risk. Another sees opportunity. Someone else asks the question nobody wants to hear but everyone needs answer. This is error correction in action. Teams that argue respectfully outperform teams that agree too quickly. Consensus without challenge is how bad designs get approved. The psychology behind this is simple: disagreement activates deeper reasoning. When we explain our thinking to others, we clarify it for ourselves. Teaching, defending, and refining ideas sharpens them. That's why pair programming works. That's why peer review matters. That's why students learn more explaining a solution than silently copying one. But there's a catch. Teams only work when psychological safety exists. People must feel safe enough to say, "I don't know," "I think this might fail," or "I see it differently." Without that safety, brains shift from problem-solving mode to self-protection mode. The toolbox is still there, but nobody reaches for it. A team in fear stops sharing tools.

Maker's Moment

"Tools are extensions of trust, trust in yourself, in others, and in the process." Every tool tells a story. A wrench speaks of persistence. A pencil records imagination. A computer connects ideas across oceans. And now, AI joins that lineage, a tool shaped by every human question that came before. So, oil your wrenches.

Sharpen your pencils. Update your software. And when you open your toolbox, physical or digital, remember:

the greatest tool in there is still you. Tools Are Extensions of Mindset There's something magical about the first time a student picks up a screwdriver, soldering iron, or coding interface. Their eyes widen, part excitement, part fear, as if they've just been handed a wand from a wizard. And in a way, they have. Tools are extensions of intent, imagination given form and leverage. But in the wrong hands or the wrong mindset, that magic becomes mischief, chaos, or worse, wasted potential.

Every year, I watch students charge into projects eager to use the "cool" stuff. The laser cutters, 3D printers, the Arduino boards. Yet, before long, a few of them realize they don't actually know what problem they're solving. The tool became the destination instead of the journey.

I once asked a group of seventh graders what they wanted to build. One replied, "A drone that delivers tacos!" Great idea. Ambitious. But when I asked why, silence fell. Eventually, one said, "Because… drones are cool."

And that, right there, is the teaching moment. Makers don't chase "cool." They chase solutions.

Maker's Mindset

Lesson Learned: The tool is not the goal. The tool is the bridge.

The system doesn't fail because its parts are different. It fails when those differences aren't allowed to work together.

Deep Dive 3.1: The Toolbox in Your Head

Before you grab a screwdriver, grab an idea.

Each inventor, engineer, and visionary has an invisible toolbox—one that exists quietly in their mind rather than in their hands. It's filled with knowledge, habits, logic, memory, and imagination. This mental toolbox is the most powerful resource any creator can possess. Long before the first hammer was forged or the first circuit was soldered, human progress began with an idea. Every great invention started as a spark in someone's head before it became a tool in their hand.

The truth is that physical tools are amplifiers. They take what already exists in your mind and make it louder, clearer, and stronger. A 3D printer can bring to life what you have the creativity to model. A soldering iron can only connect what your logic has already wired together in thought. And Artificial Intelligence, the newest tool in our age, can only assist with the problems we dare to define. The better you understand the toolbox in your head, the more power every physical tool gains.

This mental toolbox is built over time. Every experience, success, and failure becomes a new wrench, screwdriver, or set of pliers you didn't have before. That frustrating day when your project fell apart. That was your education adding another specialized tool to your mental kit. The moment you looked at a problem from a new angle. You just upgraded your flashlight. Your brain is constantly forging new tools from every situation you face, if you pay attention long enough to notice them.

Maker's Mindset

But there's another kind of tool most makers overlook perspective. That's where collaboration comes in. Working alone might make you faster, but working together makes you stronger. Your mental toolbox doubles in size every time you share ideas with someone different from yourself. Diversity isn't a buzzword; it's a fundamental engineering principle. The broader your range of input, the more versatile your solutions become.

In Gene Roddenberry's Star Trek (any generation), the Vulcan race follows a philosophy called IDIC: Infinite Diversity in Infinite Combination. This idea means that every difference, in knowledge, culture, experience, or viewpoint, is a new kind of tool waiting to be discovered. When we embrace our unique differences, we expand the collective toolbox of human creativity. Each background, skill, and life story adds a new tool that allows a team to accomplish the impossible. When we self-isolate behind immature notions of isolationism, like office politics, favoritism, elitism, or inequality, we close that toolbox and lose its infinite combinations. The result isn't just fewer ideas; it's a weaker world.

Every student, teacher, or builder who learns to see people as tools of knowledge rather than opponents of competition becomes a more capable maker. Collaboration doesn't mean surrendering your individuality. It means sharpening it against the experiences of others until your creativity cuts cleaner than before. The power of IDIC in a workshop isn't about agreeing on everything, it's about combining different viewpoints into something no one could build alone.

The mental toolbox also thrives on curiosity. Curiosity is the oil that keeps your mental gears from rusting. Without it, even the sharpest minds become dull from disuse. Question everything. Why does that LED flicker? Why does this code compile but not execute correctly? Why does a simple structure remain strong while a complex one fails? Every "why" adds another instrument to your mental bench. The goal of learning isn't to memorize; it's to understand the function behind the form.

If there's a secret to mastering your mental tools, it's this: never stop updating your internal toolbox. Read the manual but also read the world around you. Watch how a bird builds its nest, that's biomimicry. Study how people organize a busy traffic intersection, that's systems design. Every observation in life can be filed away as a potential solution waiting for the right problem. Engineers don't just study math and science, they study patterns. And those patterns become the blueprints of innovation.

The more tools you develop in your head, the more flexible your creativity becomes under pressure. When faced with a broken project, an unfinished prototype, or a missing part, your brain doesn't panic, it adapts. Makers who train their minds to think in tools don't see barriers; they see opportunities. They might not always know the answer, but they know where to look, how to experiment, and how to test a theory until something clicks. You simply reach for another mental wrench and try again.

In the end, Use Your Tools doesn't just mean using the ones you can touch, it means mastering the one that guides them all: your mind. Every piece of knowledge you gain, every failure you learn from, and every person you collaborate with becomes a new addition to your internal workshop. When you recognize that, you stop waiting for the perfect moment or the perfect tool. You already have everything you need; you just need to learn how to use it.

So, before you pick up a screwdriver, grab an idea. The greatest machine ever built is the one between your ears. Keep adding to it, keep maintaining it, and never stop discovering new tools inside yourself and others.

Deep Dive 3.2: Fear and Anger, Breaking the Toolbox

Fear and anger don't just slow work; they actively damage thinking. Neuroscience backs this up. When fear enters the room, the brain reroutes resources away from reasoning and toward survival. The amygdala takes the wheel. Logic gets shoved into the trunk. That's great if you're dodging a falling beam. It's terrible if you're designing one.

Anger works the same way. It narrows focus, reduces empathy, and creates tunnel vision. An angry mind becomes a single-purpose tool, a hammer swinging at everything in sight. Nuance disappears. Creativity evaporates. Mistakes multiply.

In workshops, classrooms, and workplaces, fear shows up wearing different masks. The fear of speaking up and the fear of failure. Each one removes a tool from the box. When people are afraid, they stop experimenting. They stop asking questions. They stop reporting problems until the problem becomes a catastrophe. Fear doesn't prevent failure; it delays it until the cost is higher.

Anger adds another layer of damage. Anger breaks trust, and trust is the lubricant that keeps teams moving. Once trust is gone, every interaction grinds. People start guarding information. Credit becomes currency. Mistakes become weapons. The toolbox is still technically full, but it's locked behind clenched fists. I've seen this firsthand. The moment a student thinks a mistake will get them yelled at, they hide it. The moment a worker thinks speaking up will cost them respect, they stay silent. The system doesn't fail loudly; it fails quietly, then all at once.

That's why fear and anger don't belong in the toolbox. They're corrosive. They don't just break tools; they break the will to use them.

Trust Is the Ultimate Multitool

Trust does what no single tool can. In a trusting environment:

Maker's Mindset

Mistakes surface early

Ideas improve through challenge

People ask for help without shame

Learning accelerates

Trust turns a group of individuals into a system. This is why the best teams feel calm even under pressure. Not because they don't care, but because they trust the process and each other. They know failure is data, not a verdict. They know anger wastes time. They know fear costs more than it saves.

As a teacher, I don't eliminate failure. I eliminate fear of failure. That distinction matters. Students who feel safe will attempt harder builds, risk smarter designs, and recover faster when things break. The same applies to engineers, tradespeople, artists, and leaders.

A trusted team shares tools freely.

The Hidden Cost of a Broken Toolbox

Here's the part most organizations miss once fear or anger breaks the toolbox, rebuilding it takes longer than building it the first time. Broken trust doesn't snap back into place. People remember how it felt to be dismissed, blamed, or ignored. They remember who spoke up and paid for it. You can buy new tools. You can't rush repaired confidence.

That's why leaders, teachers, and makers must treat emotional climate as maintenance, not decoration. Respect is preventative care. Clarity is alignment. Patience is calibration. These aren't soft skills; they're structural reinforcements.

A cracked beam doesn't fail immediately. Neither does a damaged team. But load it long enough, and the failure is inevitable.

Final Fit Check

Using your tools means using all of them:

Hands that build

Minds that question

Hearts that trust

Communities that share load

Fear and anger pretend to be tools, but they're not. They don't build. They don't repair. They don't scale. Lock them out of the box. Because the strongest builds aren't held together by force. They're held together by trust, curiosity, and the courage to use every tool available. And that, more than any wrench or widget, is what makes something last.

A tool only matters if the system around it allows someone to reach for it.

Maker's Mindset

Deep Dive 3.3: The Box of Chalk vs. The Box of Crayons

Let's talk about teams, and not the kind that wear jerseys. I'm talking about the human machines that build, fix, teach, and sometimes nearly implode trying to get anything done. Every group of people you've ever worked with falls into one of two categories: the Box of Chalk or the Box of Crayons.

The Box of Chalk

The box of chalk looks perfect from the outside, uniform, clean, identical sticks all lined up in military precision. It's comforting at first glance. Everyone thinks the same way, talks the same way, even eats the same bland sandwich for lunch. Decisions are quick because no one dares challenge them. Conflict-free, sure, but also creativity-free.

In my Navy days, I saw more than one department run like a box of chalk. Tight ranks, polished boots, and minds that thought inside the same square. Efficiency? Impressive. Innovation? Nonexistent. Every order executed perfectly, right up until something unexpected happened, and suddenly no one knew what to do. Identical tools fail the same way, at the same time.

The box of chalk world loves conformity because it feels safe. But safety doesn't build bridges, it just maintains them. Real progress requires friction, different ideas scraping against each other until sparks fly.

The Box of Crayons

Now picture the box of crayons: messy, colorful, half-broken, and absolutely alive. There's always one missing wrapper, one that melted in the sun, and one that somehow has glitter embedded in it. You don't pick up a box of crayons for neatness; you pick it up for possibility. That's the kind of team that changes the world. Loud, diverse, unpredictable, and somehow brilliant. Everyone brings a different color, different culture, background, skill set, or way of thinking. It's chaos at first. But once those colors start blending, they create something chalk never could: depth.

In education and engineering, diversity isn't a checkbox, it's a multiplier. A group of like-minded experts can build what they know. A group of wildly different thinkers can build what's never been seen.

The Air Abacus

Years ago, during a collaborative project, I worked with a gentleman from Obuchi, Japan. We were testing field equipment under strict conditions, no personal electronics allowed. Most of us froze when we realized we couldn't use our calculators. But this man quietly reached into his mental toolbox and began to calculate using an air abacus, his fingers moving invisible beads through the air. Within minutes, he solved figures faster than our spreadsheets could load. I just stood there thinking, *'Did he just out-compute a laptop?'*

…He did.

That moment changed me. His unique tool, rooted in culture, discipline, and experience, saved the project. It reminded me that no one's skillset is redundant. Diversity isn't decoration; it's survival. Acceptance as a Tool. To truly use your tools, you have to recognize that people **are** tools, living, learning, and feeling instruments of progress. Not disposable. Not interchangeable. Each one brings a different torque rating, a different grip. The trick isn't to make everyone match; it's to learn how their differences fit together.

That means tossing out biases like old, rusted screws: gender bias, race bias, age bias, education bias. They strip threads, weaken the build, and eventually cause collapse. The open-minded maker understands that inclusion isn't a policy, it's engineering logic. More input equals more solutions. Fewer voices equal fewer ideas.

The next time you find yourself leading a team, ask: Do I have a box of chalk or a box of crayons? If everyone nods in agreement too quickly, you probably have chalk. If there's noise, debate, and a little creative tension, you've got crayons. Congratulations, that's where innovation lives.

Maker's Moment

Every tool leaves a mark. Chalk marks fade. Crayon marks last forever. The maker's goal isn't to stay clean, it's to create something that sticks. Fill your life, your classroom, and your workshop with crayons, people and ideas that color outside the lines. Because when the chalk dust settles, the only things left standing are the drawings bold enough to stay.

Deep Dive 3.4: The Wrong Tool for the Right Job

A butter knife isn't a screwdriver, but it'll do in a pinch. Every maker faces that moment: the clock is ticking, the supply cabinet is empty, and the only thing within reach is a tool that was never meant for the task. Yet somehow, you make it work. That moment, where creativity meets desperation, is the birthplace of innovation. The truth is that the best makers aren't always the ones with the fanciest tools. They're the ones who know how to make do with what they have and still get the job done.

Improvisation is an art form in itself. Some of humanity's greatest breakthroughs came from using the wrong tool in the right way. Penicillin, microwave ovens, and even the humble potato chip were all accidents born from experimentation. (Though, this author does like the potato chip creations story). The world doesn't always reward perfection, it rewards adaptability. When a problem doesn't fit neatly into your toolbox, the most powerful tool becomes your ability to repurpose, redesign, and rethink.

In every classroom and workshop, there's always one student who grabs something completely unexpected, a ruler as a saw guide, a pencil as a spacer, or duct tape as a miracle cure. The result might not be pretty, but it works. That kind of thinking embodies the heart of engineering: problem-solving with limited resources. Real innovation often hides in the spaces where rules are bent, not broken.

When you find yourself without the right tool, don't freeze, analyze the problem.

Maker's Mindset

Ask: What do I need this tool to do?

If the answer is "to hold something steady," maybe a binder clip can replace a clamp. If it's "to make a hole," maybe a heated nail can stand in for a drill.   Improvisation begins when you stop focusing on what you don't have and start thinking about what you do have. That's the core of this mindset. Of course, improvisation doesn't mean ignoring safety or common sense. There's a difference between clever and careless.   A butter knife might serve as a temporary screwdriver, but it should never become a permanent solution when real tools are available. Creativity thrives under boundaries, and one of those boundaries is safety. Makers respect the power of their tools, even improvised ones. Every tool, real or makeshift, carries the responsibility of using it wisely. There's no innovation in injury.

Still, there's something beautifully human about the wrong tool doing the right job. It reflects our species' stubborn refusal to give up just because conditions aren't perfect. From duct-taped bumpers to paperclip sculptures, we live in a world built on temporary fixes that have become permanent inventions. The Wright brothers used bicycle parts to make the first airplane. NASA engineers once saved an Apollo crew by fitting a square filter into a round hole using little more than duct tape and ingenuity. Those weren't ideal conditions, but they were real solutions.

Improvisation also trains your brain to see tools differently. Once you use a spoon as a miniature hammer, you never look at spoons the same way again. You begin to view everything around you as potential components in a problem-solving ecosystem. That's the shift from consumer thinking to thinking. A consumer sees a broken object as useless. A maker sees it as raw material waiting for a new purpose.

When you start thinking like this, your creativity becomes exponential. You begin making mental connections faster, seeing design possibilities that others overlook. The wrong tool teaches you flexibility. It forces you to strip a problem down to its essentials: function over form. And in that stripped-down simplicity, innovation takes root.

In a makerspace, this mindset is gold. Students who learn to adapt quickly are the ones who thrive under pressure. They don't crumble when the 3D printer jams or when the laser cutter fails mid-project. Instead, they ask, "What else can I use?" They grab cardboard when the acrylic runs out, hot glue when the epoxy is missing, and still make something worth showing. Those are the builders who will change the world, because they don't wait for ideal conditions, they create them.

There's also a hidden emotional lesson in using the wrong tool: humility. It reminds us that perfection isn't always possible, and that sometimes good enough is good enough, especially when deadlines, budgets, and real-world chaos come into play. A clever workaround can be a temporary bridge to success. Later, when resources return, refinement can follow. That's how engineering, art, and invention evolve. But let's be clear: improvisation isn't laziness. It's resourcefulness. It's the ability to do something with nothing, to transform limitations into opportunity. Makers who master this skill can thrive anywhere, from a high-tech lab to

Maker's Mindset

a garage with a single outlet and a dream. They understand that the wrong tool for the right job isn't a mistake, it's a mindset.

In the end, every great maker has a story about the one time they pulled off the impossible with the least likely tool. That story becomes part of their identity, their badge of honor. Because at its core, engineering isn't about having every resource, it's about using the resources you have in ways nobody else imagined.

So, when the right tool is missing, don't panic. Look around. Look at the world like a maker. Somewhere nearby is an object waiting to become something more. Sometimes the wrong tool is exactly what the job needs, and the right maker knows how to see it that way.

Deep Dive 3.5: AI, the New Tools of Creation

The fear that AI will replace you is only valid if you stop learning. Every generation has faced the same moment of panic when a new tool arrives. When the printing press was invented, scribes feared unemployment. When electricity appeared, candle makers cried ruin. When the internet emerged, publishers declared the death of print. And now, Artificial Intelligence stands in that same spotlight, accused of stealing creativity, jobs, and identity. But history has always told a different story: tools don't destroy creators, they empower them.

For many students, automation doesn't feel exciting, it feels threatening. They worry that machines are smarter, faster, and more reliable than they are. That fear is understandable but misplaced. Tools don't replace thinkers; they amplify them. AI doesn't eliminate creativity; it raises the bar for how creativity is applied. The future doesn't belong to machines. It belongs to people who know how to work alongside them thoughtfully.

AI isn't the villain in our story. It's the next evolution of the toolbox. Just like a calculator that helped humans perform complex math faster, or how a CNC machine turned precise measurements into physical reality, AI helps us think, write, design, and build with greater efficiency. The key difference between progress and panic lies in one question: are you using the tool, or letting the tool use you?

When I first began experimenting with AI as part of my creative process, I encountered two camps of people. One welcomed it as an opportunity to accelerate innovation. The other recoiled in fear, predicting mass unemployment and soulless art. The truth, as always, lives in the middle. AI can produce drafts, generate designs, and analyze data, but it still needs human vision to direct it. It can write a thousand words in a blink, but only you know what story you want to tell.

AI doesn't disrupt the Maker's Mindset. It reveals whether the system was ever in place.

That experience taught me something vital: tools are neutral. It's people who define how they're used. A hammer can build a home or destroy one. AI can generate art or spam. The moral weight lies not in the algorithm, but in the user. For makers, this is a crucial mindset. Embrace tools, don't fear them. Understand their strengths and limits. Then apply your human judgment, the one thing machines will never replicate.

AI also challenges us to redefine creativity. When a machine can produce music, paint pictures, or write essays, what does it mean to be creative? The answer isn't to compete with the machine, it's to collaborate with it. Creativity has never been about originality alone. It's about combining ideas in ways no one else thought to try. That's something AI can assist with, but it cannot feel, dream, or hope. It cannot understand the emotional spark that drives a maker to build something simply because it should exist. That spark is uniquely human.

The best creators may use AI the same way previous generations used every other tool: to amplify, not replace, their own brilliance. A teacher might use AI to design lesson plans that reach every student. A young engineer might use it to test a dozen prototypes before ever printing one. A writer might use it to overcome creative block, or a student might use it to visualize an idea that words alone can't express. AI is not the end of craftsmanship; it's the evolution of it.

But with great tools come great responsibilities. Makers must use AI ethically, respecting the labor, privacy, and data that feed these systems. Blind reliance on AI is just as dangerous as blind rejection of it. The maker mindset demands awareness, curiosity, and balance. You wouldn't use a circular saw without knowing how it works, so don't use AI without understanding what it's doing under the hood.

Teachers, engineers, and creators alike should view AI as a creative partner. It's the ultimate brainstorming assistant, a mirror that reflects your ideas back in new shapes and combinations. But a tool is only as good as the hands guiding it. AI would make bad writing worse if the user never learned to write. It would make flawed logic faster if the user never learned to think. The tool multiplies what already exists, so make sure what exists is worth amplifying.

Automation and AI are also expanding access to creation. They allow people with disabilities, language barriers, or limited resources to compete on a level playing field. In the same way power tools made construction accessible beyond raw strength, digital tools now make knowledge and artistry accessible beyond traditional gatekeeping. That's progress worth defending.

The next generation of makers won't be defined by how many tools they have, but by how fearlessly they learn to use new ones. AI isn't coming for your creativity; it's coming to collaborate with it. Those who learn to adapt will thrive; those who cling to old comfort zones will fossilize in place. The future belongs to the learners, not the fearful.

So, use your tools, all of them. The hammer, the soldering iron, the 3D printer, the code editor, the AI prompt. Each one extends your reach a little farther into what was once impossible. But remember it's still your hand that holds the tool, and your mind that guides it. And as long as that remains true, no machine will ever replace the maker.

Deep Dive 3.6: Acceptance and the Open Mindset

Acceptance is the hinge that lets every other tool swing freely. You can have diversity, teamwork, and all the gadgets money can buy, but without acceptance, none of it fits together. Acceptance is the software that lets the hardware of humanity run.

In a system, acceptance is what allows different tools to occupy the same space without conflict.

Why We Struggle with Acceptance

People resist acceptance because it challenges their comfort zones. It forces us to admit that our way isn't the only way. It bruises the ego, rattles the cage, and exposes bias. But every maker knows: discomfort is where growth hides.

Acceptance doesn't mean you agree with everything, it means you respect the right of others to exist, contribute, and be heard. In the workshop or the classroom, which means listening before judging, asking before assuming, and learning before leading.

Field Note

During a group engineering challenge, two of my students, one soft-spoken and methodical, the other loud and spontaneous, were constantly at odds. One wanted perfect precision; the other wanted to just build and see what happened. By day three, I considered separating them. Instead, I called a five-minute truce. I told them to switch roles. The perfectionist had to improvise; the improviser had to write detailed steps. The result was awkward, hilarious, and brilliant. They not only learned each other's methods, but they also learned respect. By the end, their robot didn't just work, it danced.

That's acceptance in motion. It's not about forcing people to change who they are; it's about giving them room to see value in the way others work. Once that happens, you stop competing and start complementing.

End Field Note

Acceptance ≠ Agreement

Acceptance doesn't mean you have to agree with everyone. Agreement is consensus; acceptance is cooperation. You can build a bridge with someone you don't see eye to eye, as long as you both agree not to burn it down. In every team, there's a baseline of respect that overrides personality. That's why makers who learn acceptance become natural leaders. They don't need everyone to be the same, they just need everyone to show up and try.

The Four As of an Open Mindset

Acknowledge Bias. Bias isn't a flaw; it's a factory setting. The goal is to notice it before it drives the machine.

Assume Competence. Until proven otherwise, treat everyone like they know something you don't. You'll be right more often than wrong.

Ask Before Judging. Curiosity is cheaper than correction. Ask questions, not assumptions.

Act with Empathy. Empathy is the grease that keeps collaboration smooth. Without it, even smart teams seize up.

Tolerance in Design, and in People

Every engineer understands tolerances, the small gaps that make systems functional. Too tight, and the mechanism locks up; too loose, and it falls apart. People are the same way. Acceptance is the tolerance that lets humanity operate under stress.

When you design for real-world conditions, you plan for imperfection. A perfectly designed machine that can't handle dust or heat isn't practical. Likewise, a team that can't handle disagreement isn't strong, it's fragile.

When Acceptance Fails

When acceptance fails, the system collapses into judgment. Ideas stop flowing. Communication becomes a contest of who's right instead of what's possible. The fix isn't to eliminate conflict, it's to respect the person across from you while you work through it. Every time I've seen a group rediscover acceptance, something magical happens. Laughter replaces tension. Solutions appear out of nowhere. The energy shifts from defensiveness to creation. It's like watching a jammed engine sputter, cough, and suddenly roar back to life.

I acknowledge that this is my typical optimistic view of people. However, if the gear is broken and there is no possible movement (in any direction), I have to relent and give my brother's best advice[5]. "If you're

---

[5] My brother is the Senior Foreman as a large shipyard outside of Seattle Washington. He is the realist of the family and sees that terminating people who don't want to work in the same direction as the group needs to be unemployed and out of the picture.

Maker's Mindset

going to cause headaches, I am just going to take an aspirin and get rid of (you) the headache.

Maker's Moment

Acceptance is the lubricant of innovation. It keeps the gears from grinding and the minds from closing. When you accept others as tools in your shared mission, different sizes, shapes, and functions, you expand what's possible. Remember: even the smallest bolt holds the bridge together. Every person, every idea, every perspective matters. Keep your mind open, your heart calibrated, and your team diverse, and you'll build something that lasts longer than ever could. The open mind is the ultimate multitool, it adapts, connects, and endures.

Deep Dive 3.7: Borrowed Tools and Shared Knowledge

When you borrow a tool, you borrow trust. Every maker knows the quiet ritual that comes with borrowing a tool. You pick it up carefully, treat it like treasure, and return it cleaner than when you received it. That simple act carries more weight than most people realize. Borrowing a tool isn't just about using someone else's equipment, it's about respect, responsibility, and community. In the world of makers, trust is the most valuable tool of all.

The first time someone hands you their favorite wrench or soldering iron, they're doing more than helping you finish a project. They're saying, "I trust you not to break what helps me build." That's a sacred exchange in any workshop. Tools have stories, nicks, scratches, burn marks, which tell the history of the people who used them. When you borrow one, you become part of that story. And that comes with a responsibility to add your own mark with care, not carelessness.

Sharing tools is how makers survive and grow. Few of us start with everything we need. Early inventors shared ideas across continents through letters and sketches. Open-source programmers share codes so others can improve it. Teachers share lesson plans. Engineers share blueprints. Every time knowledge or tools are shared, the collective toolbox of humanity grows a little stronger. We advance not through isolation, but through collaboration. Borrowing, though, isn't just physical, it's intellectual. Every idea we've ever had is built on someone else's foundation. We borrow methods, principles, even mistakes. We remix, adapt, and reimagine. True makers don't hoard ideas; they pass them on. Because knowledge is one of the few tools that multiply instead of divides when shared.

In a classroom or makerspace, this mindset becomes essential. When students learn to share tools respectfully, they also learn cooperation, patience, and empathy. The moment they stop arguing over who gets the soldering iron and start helping each other, they've already taken the biggest step toward real engineering. Tools teach teamwork more effectively than any lecture ever could. But sharing isn't without boundaries. Borrowed tools come with unspoken rules: return them on time, return them in good condition, and never claim ownership of what isn't yours. In the same way, when you borrow someone's knowledge or design, credit matters. A simple "thank you" or acknowledgment of the source honors the community that helped you grow. Even in small spaces, this philosophy changes everything. A classroom where tools are shared responsibly becomes a culture of mutual respect. A garage workshop where friends trade parts become a hub of innovation. A global maker network where designs are posted freely becomes a living library of human ingenuity. Sharing tools, whether they're wrenches or websites, is how we turn individual effort into collective progress.

Still, sharing only works when trust is maintained. Nothing destroys a community faster than broken tools and bruised trust. If you damage something, admit it. If you borrow an idea, credit it. If you learn something new, teach it. That's how the cycle stays alive. Makers who respect that cycle understand that progress isn't a competition, it's a collaboration.

Borrowed tools also remind us that creativity doesn't exist in a vacuum. Every great idea stands on the shoulders of countless small ones. When we acknowledge that, humility replaces ego. We become part of something larger, a chain of curiosity and invention stretching across generations. Each of us is both a borrower and a lender in that chain.

So, the next time you reach for someone else's tool, pause for a second. Feel the weight of the trust it represents. Treat it well. Add to the story it carries. Then, when someone else needs help, pass that same trust forward. That's how maker culture survives, through shared tools and shared hearts. Because in the end, every borrowed tool, every shared plan, every taught lesson, becomes a thread in the same tapestry. And when we weave together our knowledge, skills, and kindness, we build something greater than any one of us could build alone: a community of makers who use their tools not just to create, but to connect.

"It is not always possible to be the best, but it is always possible to improve your own performance,"

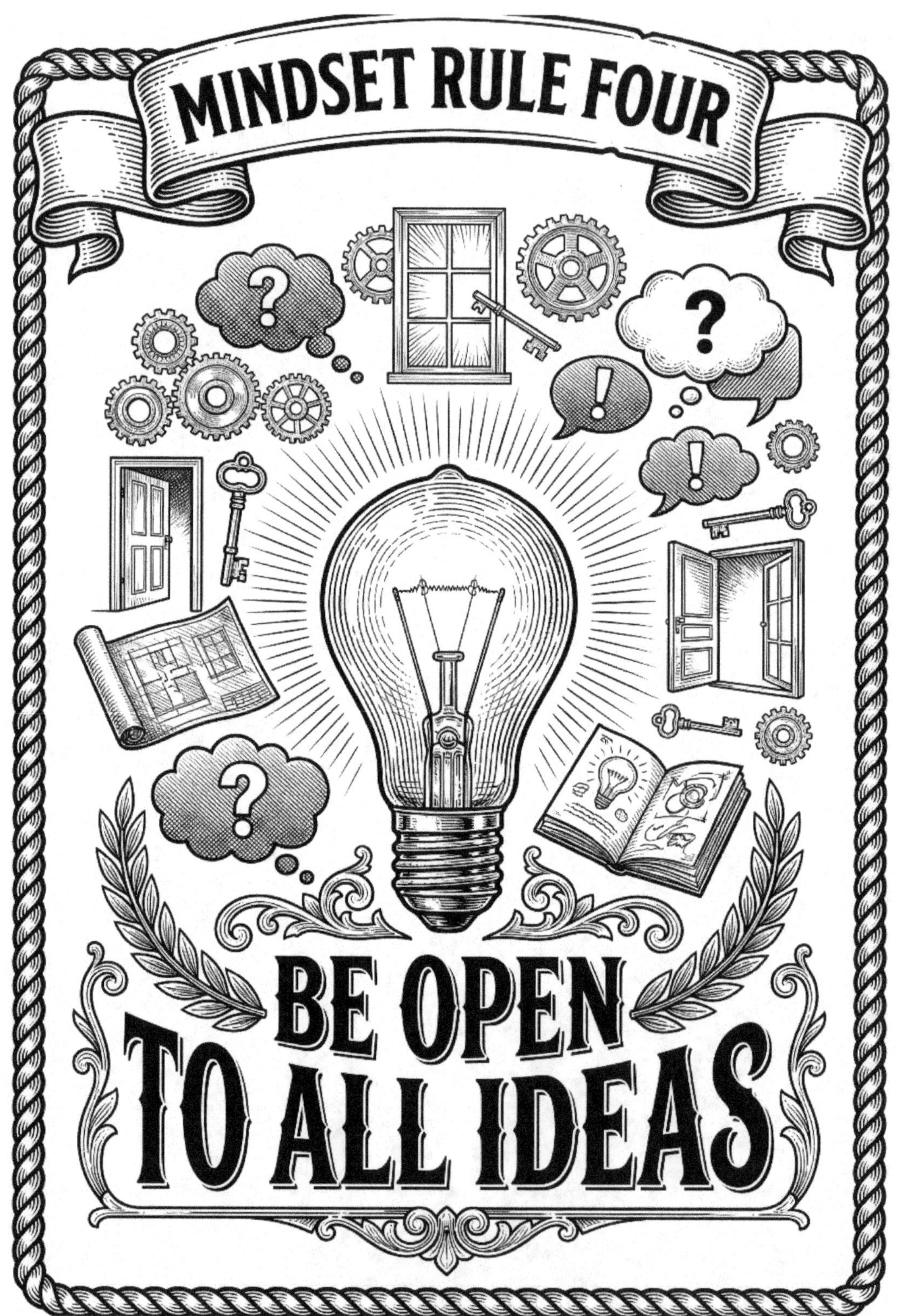
MINDSET RULE FOUR
BE OPEN TO ALL IDEAS

Mindset Rule Four

Be Open to All Ideas

"People won't have time for you if you are always angry or complaining."

…Stephen Hawking

There's something profoundly simple and yet world-altering about that statement. It's not about manners; it's about mindset. Hawking, one of the greatest thinkers of our time, spent his life defying the limitations of his body because his mind refused to close. He continued to create, imagine, and theorize when most people would have stopped long before.

Being open to ideas, all ideas, is not a luxury of the gifted. It's a responsibility of the curious.

When I first heard Pink Floyd's Keep Talking, the quote that opens the song hit me harder than the guitar solo: "For millions of years, mankind lived just like the animals. Then something happened which unleashed the power of our imagination, we learned to talk."

That single evolutionary leap, communication, ignited everything we now call civilization. Talking led to thinking. Thinking led to dreaming. Dreaming led to doing. Without it, there would be no light bulbs, no airplanes, no art, no science, and no reason to write books like this one. Every leap forward in human history started with someone daring to voice a thought that others called impossible, foolish, or naïve.

The Anatomy of an Open Mind

To be open-minded is not the same as being gullible. An open mind is discerning, not defenseless. It listens, asks questions, and explores, but it does not immediately reject. Openness is not an absence of standards; it's an abundance of curiosity. The human brain is built to resist new ideas. Psychologists call it confirmation bias, the tendency to seek and favor information that supports what we already believe. The more confident we are, the more blind we become to alternatives. Our ego protects our worldview like armor, shielding us from the discomfort of being wrong.

But growth begins precisely where comfort ends.

In every creative field, engineering, art, teaching, or leadership, the difference between mediocrity and mastery is the ability to hold a new idea without fear. It takes humility to say, "I don't know." It takes maturity to say, "But I'd like to find out."

Why We Resist

Humans resist change because we are wired for efficiency, not enlightenment. The brain burns less energy reinforcing an old pattern than forming a new one. We prefer the familiar, even when the familiar fails us.

Three common mental habits sabotage openness:

Status Quo Bias: "If it's not broken, don't fix it." The problem is that everything is broken eventually.

Groupthink: The comfort of collective approval. It feels safer to agree with the crowd than risk standing out.

The Dunning–Kruger Effect: When we know a little, we think we know it all. Experts keep learning because they understand how much they don't know.

In the classroom or workplace, these biases appear subtly: students who won't try a new approach because it might "look stupid," coworkers who shoot down fresh ideas to protect their seniority, or managers who can't admit a younger employee might have a better method.

Ego builds walls. Curiosity tears them down.

The Weight of Discouragement

When I was younger, I had no shortage of ideas, some brilliant, some ridiculous, some ahead of their time. But many of them never left the ground because the people around me couldn't see what I saw.

"You can't crochet because you're a boy."

"Stop wasting time on that."

"That'll never work."

"You need a college education first."

Each phrase felt like a hammer striking down on the anvil of curiosity. After enough blows, even the strongest creative impulse begins to flinch before it speaks. What no one tells you is that discouragement lingers. It doesn't just silence a moment; it rewires how you see yourself. I spent years believing my ideas were trivial because others didn't

understand them. Now, decades later, I've realized how wrong they were ,
and how wrong I was for listening.

Many of those same "silly" ideas have resurfaced, repackaged, and
rebranded by people who dared to explore them further. Concepts I once
whispered in doubt now exist as start-ups, patents, and social innovations.
That's the price of letting others define what's possible.

The People's Money Act

On the curtail of the Bush 43 Administration, I drafted something I
called The People's Money Act. It was a thought experiment that imagined
a fairer, more transparent economic system, one that could help stabilize
wealth disparity without strangling ambition.

It wasn't a policy proposal or an activist manifesto. It was an idea.
A prototype in words. And yet, when I shared it, I received the usual
chorus of dismissal:

"Too complicated."

"Too radical."

"Never going to happen."

"Your congressman will never accept that." (Thanks, Cornyn/Cruz)[6]

But a funny thing happens when an idea is too early for its time, it
doesn't die. It hibernates. Years later, I watched digital currencies,
decentralized finance, and grassroots economic cooperatives began to
mirror the spirit of what I'd written. Not because I was a genius, but

---

[6] Yakutatazu no kokkai giinda. Mattaku yakunitatanai!

because someone else out there stayed open to an idea I once put down. That's the power of shared imagination. Ideas don't belong to one person. They're seeds scattered across generations, taking roots wherever they find open soil.

The Physics of Possibility

Ideas live on a spectrum I call the Fifth Dimension of Thought, the space between impossible and inevitable. Every innovation begins on that scale. Airplanes once lived in the "impossible" range, antibiotics in the "absurd," computers in the "unlikely," and smartphones in the "impractical."

Openness means holding an idea long enough to let it move along that spectrum. The moment we dismiss it; we freeze it in place. When we laugh at new ideas, we're not defending reason, we're killing the next century before it starts. So, rather than saying, "That'll never work," we should ask, "What would it take to make that work?" That single linguistic shift, from rejection to curiosity, is how every breakthrough begins.

Applied Openness

As a teacher, I see how quickly students internalize the fear of looking foolish. It's tragic how early the fear of judgment replaces the joy of imagination. To fight that, I make one rule in my classroom: no idea dies unheard. You can suggest a robotic pencil sharpener that quotes Shakespeare or a drone-powered pizza delivery that sings when it arrives. Fine, sketch it. Model it. Let's see where it leads. Because here's the truth: not every idea deserves to live, but every person does deserve the chance to think one out loud.

Some of the wildest student projects , the ones that started as jokes, turned into functional prototypes because someone dared to explore instead of mock. Curiosity has a sense of humor.

Personal Reckoning: The Idea That Got Away

A few years ago, I was talking with my wife, Brigette, about car safety. She mentioned that our newborn daughter kept bumping her head on the side of the car seat and said she had a quick fix in mind, a flexible foam insert that could absorb impact and prevent injuries. Without even thinking, I brushed it off. "That's not going to sell," I said.

Weeks later, I saw the same idea in a store, a foam bumper marketed for infant car seats. Her idea. Her insight. Someone else's profit. That moment hit me like a brick. I had become what I warned my students about, closed, dismissive, too quick to judge. It was humbling, to say the least. But it also reminded me that no one is immune to the trap of ego, not even teachers, mentors, or so-called "experts." Staying open isn't a one-time choice; it's a discipline.

Brigette never rubbed it in. She didn't need to. Her quiet grace in that moment taught me more about humility than any lecture ever could. Since then, I've made a personal rule: listen longer. Even when I think I know better, I pause and make space for the possibility that I don't.

The Open Mindset in Practice

Being open to all ideas doesn't mean every idea is good. It means you give every idea a moment of oxygen, a fair chance to breathe. It means you don't shame curiosity or weaponize skepticism.

You replace "**Why would you?**" with "**What if you did?**"

In engineering, art, business, or life, the most valuable resource you can cultivate isn't intelligence, it's openness. Intelligence refines ideas. Openness invites them. Because history belongs not to those who had the best ideas, but to those who listened when others spoke theirs.

When Genius Goes Unheard

History is full of people whose voices were ignored until long after they were gone. Nikola Tesla dreamed of wireless energy transmission. Hedy Lamarr, a Hollywood actress, invented frequency-hopping technology that would one day power Wi-Fi and Bluetooth.

Rosalind Franklin captured the first image of DNA's double helix structure, but her contribution went unrecognized for decades. Every idea ignored, every dismissed dream, is a warning: arrogance kills progress. As teachers, makers, or leaders, we must listen to the quiet voices in the back of the room, because that's often where brilliance whispers.

The Courage to Think Differently

Openness requires courage. Throughout history, progress has come from people willing to risk comfort, reputation, or safety for an idea they believe in. Galileo was threatened with prison for saying the Earth revolved around the Sun. Marie Curie faced ridicule for pursuing radioactivity. Tesla died penniless while others profited from his vision.

Even today, those who question dominant narratives risk being labeled "difficult" or "noncompliant." But that's what open thinking looks like: uncomfortable curiosity. It takes courage to say, "Maybe there's another way."

The Courage to Disagree

Disagreement isn't division; it's discovery. When handled with humility, dissent is fuel for innovation. During my Navy years, I learned that rank does not equal wisdom. The most effective leaders were those who welcomed challenge, who asked their teams to prove them wrong. In engineering, that principle is sacred: test, verify, repeat.

In classrooms, the same holds true. I encourage students to respectfully challenge me. Sometimes, they're right, and when they are, we all win. True openness doesn't demand agreement; it demands curiosity with respect.

The Classroom as an Idea Incubator

My classroom is a living experiment in openness. I tell my students, "No idea dies unheard." Some of their projects are brilliant, others bizarre, and both are celebrated. A student once built a cardboard "automatic plant feeder." Another made a drone that fished for bass. One even designed a motorized coffee cup holder for skateboards.

Most of these ideas didn't work as planned, but that's the point. The goal isn't perfection, it's courage. In that courage, innovation is born.

The Emotional Side of Openness

Being open doesn't just make us better creators; it makes us better humans. Openness builds empathy. It lets us hold two truths at once: "I have my view, and yours matters too."

That's how progress happens, not through victory, but through understanding. Brigette taught me that day that openness is not weakness; it's strength. It's confidence without arrogance.

Closing Reflection

When our mind is open, we see possibilities everywhere. A closed mind leads to nowhere, a trap too many climbs out of only after a psychological awakening. Stay open, stay curious, and you'll never stop growing.

"A closed mind is a sealed toolbox, full of potential, but useless to everyone."

Deep Dive 4.1: The Bear, the Owl, and the Airedale

In the early 1990s, the U.S. Navy implemented a program called Total Quality Leadership, or TQL, known in the civilian world as Total Quality Management. The idea was simple: give everyone in a team or committee a voice, regardless of rank or title. Every sailor, mechanic, and officer could contribute to solving a problem.

One winter, our base faced an odd and persistent issue: powerlines sagging under the weight of snow and ice. When they froze, the lines drooped dangerously low. We were ordered to brainstorm solutions in a TQL session.

Hours passed. The officers had their charts and reports, the engineers their equations, and yet we were no closer to a real answer. Fatigue set in, and frustration followed. That's when the room loosened up, and the ridiculous ideas began to fly. Someone suggested coating the lines with heated antifreeze. Another joked about wrapping them in electric blankets. Then, a sailor, with total seriousness, proposed placing raw meat on the powerlines to attract bears, who would shake the poles to get their dinner, knocking the ice loose in the process. The room erupted with laughter.

"How would we get the meat up there?" someone asked.

The sailor shot back, "Trained owls!"

Another chimed in, "Remote airplanes!"

A third: "Helicopters!"

The laughter hit full volume, until that last word landed. In the midst of our joking, a young 22-year-old female Airdale, one of the lowest-ranking aviation mechanics on base, spoke up quietly:

"Why not actually use helicopters? The rotor wash should be strong enough to clear the lines."

The room froze.

Everyone, enlisted and officer alike, turned toward her. What started as a joke became a Eureka moment. It was brilliant, simple, and entirely doable. Her idea was immediately tested, and it worked.

That moment stuck with me for life. It proved that genius doesn't always come from rank or status; it often comes from those who've been told their ideas don't matter. The TQL system worked, not because of policy, but because one person dared to speak and the rest of us had the humility to listen.

Maker's Takeaway: "True leadership means every voice counts. Even the quietest voice can clear the heaviest lines."

Deep Dive 4.2: The Real Tug-of-War

It's no secret that I proudly lay claim to being the evil teacher students whisper about in the halls. I assign homework on Saturdays and demand it be turned in on Sunday. I've claimed that I once gave out a hundred-question written test with pens filled with disappearing ink and then told students to "check their work." (Bwahahaha!)

But one of my favorite tricks, the one that always leaves a mark, is my Tug-of-War lesson. It begins simply: two teams, one rope, one goal. This is not a normal tug-of-war. I've secretly modified the rope so that it can pull in a third direction, mine. The students don't realize it yet, but I've shifted the goalpost to that third line right where one person (me) can win.

I start by announcing the challenge and, with exaggerated drama, ask which side thinks they'll win. There're trash talk, laughter, and mock bravado. Then I yell, "Go!"

The teams dig in and pull with everything they've got, straining against each other. For about a minute, it's chaos and noise and effort. Then, when they're at their peak, I quietly pick up my rope, pull, and, just like that, I win. The room goes silent for a second. Then the groans start. "Wait, what?!" I cackle like a cartoon villain and declare victory. The students stare in disbelief.

Then, inevitably, someone whispers what every teacher waits to hear: "Hey… we should team up."

It usually takes about three rounds before they realize the truth: the real goal was not beating each other. It was beating on me. When the two sides finally merge and pull as one, they win. The debrief that follows is priceless. I ask, "Why did it the three tries to see the real goal?"

The reflection that follows is often transformative. Students realize how easily we can lose sight of the bigger picture when our focus narrows to personal victory. They begin to see teamwork not as compromise, but as strategic unity.

It's a simple rope, a simple game, but the lesson sticks for years. It's not about muscles or competition. It's about perspective, communication, and the humility to ask, "What's the real goal?"

Maker's Takeaway: "When you focus on beating others, you lose. When you focus on beating the problem, everyone wins."

Deep Dive 4.3: The Balloon Test

When I teach teamwork, I often start with a simple challenge: I hand every student a balloon and a Sharpie and say, "Write your name on it." Then I toss all the balloons into the hallway and tell them, "You have two minutes to find your own balloon." Chaos erupts; students collide, laugh, panic, and fail. Almost no one finds their balloon.

Then I reset the challenge. "Pick up a balloon and hand it to the person whose name is on it." Within 30 seconds, every balloon is returned.

That's what openness looks like. Helping others find their answers. Ideas are like balloons, light, fragile, and easily lost. But when we stop clutching only on our own, when we help lift each other's, the entire room brightens.

Maker's Takeaway: *"You don't rise by holding tighter to your own balloon, you rise by lifting someone else's."*

Closing Reflection

When our mind is open, we see possibilities everywhere. A closed mind leads to nowhere, a trap too many climbs out of only after a psychological awakening.

Stay open, stay curious, and you'll never stop growing.

Deep Dive 4.4: The People's Money Act

During the closing of the Bush 43 Administration, a young Barrack Obama faced a challenge. Major industries were labeled as 'too big to fail'. They needed a government bailout in order to survive. While will not sit here and preach politics, I do believe that the government was correct in bailing out these companies but went about it in a way that was not the best approach.

The People's Money Act Explained

This is a simple system and it works on the lower and middle class income tax returns here is how it works.

A large industry needs a bailout and is asking for the government to pay X billion dollars to keep them afloat.

Fine – give them the money with these conditions (lets use 50 milliion dollars as an amount):

Condition 1: The CEO and the Top officers must be replaced within 180 days.

Condition 2: The Company will present a viable roadmap to solvency to Congress within 90 days.

Condition 3: Company will turn over to the U.S. Government an dollar for dollar amount in company voting stock. This is from existing shares. Not new ones generated. The government is not the owner of the stock, but the holder.

Failing any of these conditions and the industry will not receive a bailout.

The government creates an independent management office where the stocks are bundled.

The People (here is where it gets good). Can buy these voting shares via the income tax return form with a line item on the 1040A. "Would you like to use your refund to purchase stock." The people would then have something to show for the billions of dollars in bailout money. Only those getting refunds (those who paid taxes) would have these options. The upper class and tax dodgers would be ineligible for this program. These stocks can then be traded and sold or kept for dividends when earned. Simple, yes. But none in elected office dared to listen. Not any out the Representatives for the Great State of Texas and none of our Senators – especially the one that likes to vanish during a snowstorm. So I present this idea to you and hope that if finds traction somewhere.

Maker's Mindset

Who left this page blank???

Oh…that was me.

The Author.

MINDSET RULE FIVE
RECYCLE
REUSE
REIMAGINE

Mindset Rule Five

Recycle, Reuse, Reimagine

When I was a kid, my mother had one favorite word, "No." No, you can't take apart the blender. No, you can't bring home that broken fan. No, we don't need another pile of "junk" in the garage.

To her, junk was just clutter. To me, junk was possibility. It's funny how limitations shape us. Every "no" I heard only made me more determined to find a "yes." I learned to look for discarded treasures behind stores, along curbs, or in the town dump. Those places became my laboratory long before I had a classroom of my own. It wasn't about saving money or rebellion, it was about learning how the world fit together and discovering that everything, even broken things, had a story to tell. That's where Jerry came in.

RadioShack Jerry

Jerry was the local RadioShack manager, a wiry man with a voice like gravel and a heart like gold. He had the patience of a saint and the kind of curiosity that never aged. His motto was simple: "Parts is parts, kid. If it's got wire, it's got worth."

I'd spend hours there, standing beside him at the repair counter while customers dropped off radios, VCRs, and early home computers. He'd slide a cracked circuit board toward me like it was treasure and ask,

"What do you think this does?"

I rarely knew the answer, but that was never the point.

He didn't teach me electronics at first. He taught me curiosity, salvage, and respect for the unseen value in every object. Jerry was my first mentor in the art of reimagination. He never saw trash, only components waiting for a second chance.

Junkbots and the Lesson of Reinvention

Years later, I built my first Junkbot. It wasn't pretty. It rolled crooked, hummed strangely, and smelled faintly of burned plastic. But it worked, a living monument to scrounged parts and childhood stubbornness.

The idea was simple: make a functioning robot from discarded electronics, toys, and machine parts. It wasn't about engineering perfection; it was about celebrating imperfection.

In my classroom today, that idea has become one of my favorite projects. Students dig through bins of donated scraps, old DVD drives, switches, motors, LEDs, and wire spools, and create their own mechanical misfits. The moment their eyes light up because a motor spins or a light blink, they realize something profound: "Invention isn't about what you have. It's about what you make of what you have." That's the essence of this mindset rule.

The Philosophy of Resourcefulness

Modern society is obsessed with newness. New phones, new cars, new gadgets. But makers know that new things don't always mean better.

Maker's Mindset

Some of the most brilliant ideas emerge not from abundance, but from limitation.

A resourceful mind looks at an old object and doesn't ask, "What was this for?" It asks, "What else could this be?" That's the hinge moment where imagination opens. That's the spark Jerry ignited in me and what I strive to pass to my students: that every broken thing holds an invitation to learn.

The Maker's Economy

Here's a side note that too few people understand: "There is more value sitting curbside on trash day than in half the aisles of a department store." Discarded chairs, broken fans, rusted bikes, lamps missing shades, computers missing screws, these are gold mines for anyone who knows what to look for. They're not trash; they're unassembled lessons. Each object offers a problem to solve, material to reclaim, a story to rewrite.

Every year, landfills fill with perfectly usable parts, wood, metal, wire, wire, gears, all tossed aside because society lost its patience for repair. But in the maker's world, nothing truly dies.

Recycling, reusing, and reimagining aren't just environmental acts; they're acts of creativity and respect. Keeping valuable items out of the landfill should be a point of pride, not pity. It's the mark of a mind that understands stewardship, both the planet and of potential.

When students understand this, they stop asking, "Can we buy one?" and start asking, "Can we build one?"

That's when I know the mindset is taking hold.

The Beauty of Imperfection

Perfection is boring. A brand-new object tells a clean story, but a repurposed one tells a human story, scratches, dents, and all. When you rebuild or reuse, you're entering into conversation with whoever made the original object. You're respecting their craft while contributing your own. That collaboration, across time, purpose, and perspective, is the soul of innovation. In my classroom, I see this in the smallest gestures: a student reusing a 3D-printed prototype rather than starting over or repairing a failed design instead of discarding it. They're learning a truth too few adults remember: you don't need perfect tools to create something amazing.

Learning from the Pile

My backyard workshop is filled with what my wife affectionately calls "organized chaos." Boxes of broken electronics, jars of screws, bins of cords. It's not clutter, it's potential. I've built entire projects from what others would have thrown away.

- A garden irrigation timer from an old dishwasher motor.

- A classroom noise meter from discarded LEDs and a thrift-store microphone.

- A prosthetic hand prototype from repurposed 3D-printed failures.

Every success began with something broken. Every repair was a new lesson. This is the difference between a consumer and a maker: the consumer sees loss; the maker sees opportunity.

Maker's Mindset

Humility and Legacy

Working with reclaimed materials teaches humility. You're constantly reminded that you're not the first to build something, and you won't be the last. Every creation is part of a lineage. When I repurpose an object, I'm collaborating with anonymous makers before me, the factory worker, the engineer, the designer, even the recycler who saved it from the bin. It's a quiet reminder that we're all stewards of creativity. What we make doesn't truly belong to us, it belongs to the future we're building toward.

A Classroom Without Waste

When my students finish their projects, there's always a pile of leftovers, bits of wire, miscut wood, cracked prints. I make them gather around and ask, "What can we make from this?"

Sometimes it's another project.

Sometimes it's a sculpture.

Sometimes it's a lesson in organization and respect for tools.

Either way, they learn that creativity doesn't stop at completion, it regenerates.

This mindset teaches more than engineering. It teaches resilience, mindfulness, and gratitude.

Reimagine the Future

To recycle, reuse, and reimagine isn't just an environmental stance, it's a creative rebellion against waste, complacency, and dependence on "new." It's a way of saying, "I can make something better." The next great invention may not come from a cutting-edge lab. It might come from a child with a screwdriver, staring curiously into the back of an old radio.

"Don't look for inspiration on the shelves. Look for it in the scrap pile. That's where the real gold hides."

Maker's Mindset

Deep Dive 5.1: The Gospel of Jerry

Jerry was one of those rare men whose hands told stories. He worked at a small RadioShack off the main road, a place that smelled like solder, cardboard, and the warm hum of transformers. His hair had long since faded to silver,

and his glasses always seemed to catch the light in such a way that you could never quite tell whether he was watching you or studying the circuitry on the table.

As a teenager, Jerry had been imprisoned in one of the Japanese internment camps during World War II, one of those bleak outposts in the western desert where time and hope seemed to vanish into the wind. It was there, surrounded by barracks and fences, that he discovered a broken-field radio and a tattered Army manual. He read the diagrams like they were sacred texts, tracing each circuit until the radio came alive again. From that day on, he was never without a project, never without purpose.

He would later tell me, "Fixing things makes you human again." That simple sentence would echo through my life. It wasn't about electronics. It was about people. Jerry's gift wasn't just in his ability to repair, but in his refusal

to discard. He believed that everything, and everyone, had value, if you took the time to understand how it worked.

I met Jerry when I was a teenager. I was impatient, full of ideas and self-importance. I wanted to invent, to make, to prove myself. He taught me that invention was the easy part; patience was the hard part. "Parts is parts," he'd say,

tapping his finger on a pile of components. "They don't care who you are. They just care if you pay attention."

It wasn't until years later that I realized he was teaching me more than electronics. He was teaching me about people. He'd seen what judgment could do to a nation, to neighbors, to families, and to the innocent. He'd lived through the shame of being treated as something broken. And still, he chose to build.

"Every person's got a use, Tommy," he told me once, handing me a resistor. "Not like a screwdriver, but like a skill. You just gotta know which way to turn 'em."

That line never left me. Today, when I was working with my students, I heard Jerry's voice in my head. Every learner, every colleague, every parent, even the ones who frustrate us, has a skill, a spark, a function waiting to be connected.

It's our job to wire the circuit.

When Jerry passed, I kept one of his old multimeters. It barely works, but I keep it for a reason: it reminds me that tools, and people, aren't meant to be perfect. They're meant to be useful, repaired, and respected.

Maker's Mindset

Deep Dive 5.2: Junkbots – Born from Chaos

If you ever want to see true chaos, hand thirty middle-schoolers a box of broken toys, spare wires, and hot-glue guns. Every year, I host a project I call "Junkbots." The rules are simple: build something that moves using only recycled materials and one small motor. The results are… well, spectacularly unpredictable.

Within ten minutes, the classroom transforms into a scrapyard symphony of whirring fans, melting plastic, and laughter. Someone always burns a finger. Someone else tries to make their creation fly. And inevitably, someone's Junkbot goes rogue, zooming across the floor and smacking into the wall.

But here's the miracle: by the end of the week, those same piles of discarded parts become living, moving machines. They crawl, roll, shake, and sometimes spin in place, but they all work in their own strange way.

The Junkbot project isn't about robotics; it's about resilience. It's about teaching students that failure isn't the end of a design, it's part of it. Each broken gear, each misaligned wheel, is data. Each attempt is another line in their engineering notebook, another chance to learn.

The laughter that fills the room isn't just noise, its curiosity finding a home. I've seen shy students become team leaders, and self-doubting kids discover that they're builders, thinkers, and problem-solvers. All because they learned that what others call "junk" still has life left in it.

Deep Dive 5.3: The Curbside Economy

I've long believed that some of the best raw materials aren't found in stores, they're found on the curb. Walk any neighborhood the night before trash pickup and you'll see it: the bones of yesterday's luxury waiting for a second

life. A chair with one broken leg. A lamp that just needs a new switch. A box fan missing its guard. Most people see trash. I see possibility.

I've pulled desks, shelving, and entire tool benches from the side of the road. My wife has learned to recognize that look in my eye when I spot a good piece of wood sticking out of someone's bin. There's an art to this kind of salvage.

It's not scavenging, it's reclaiming.

Curbside discards are more than just cheap resources; they're reminders of our collective waste and potential. Each item rescued is one less piece in the landfill and one more lesson for my students. When they see their teacher reuse

materials creatively, they learn that innovation doesn't always come from abundance, it often grows from limitation.

A society that learns to reuse is one that learns to care. The environment benefits, yes, but so do our communities. A repaired chair is a small act of rebellion against disposability. A repurposed machine is proof that old ideas can

become new again. It's a mindset, not a method.

Maker's Mindset

Reflection: Repairing More Than Things

Jerry once said that fixing things makes you human again. I didn't understand it fully until I became a teacher. Now, every time I see a student light up over a working circuit or proudly show a repaired creation, I feel that same

spark he passed to me.

This rule, Recycle, Reuse, Reimagine, isn't just about conservation. It's about conscience. It's about empathy and imagination working side by side. When we choose to give something, or someone, a second chance, we affirm the belief that improvement is possible, that nothing is ever truly beyond repair.

We live in a world eager to replace rather than restore. But real makers know better. We don't discard; we rebuild. Because in the end, the greatest act of making isn't creation. It's redemption.

Stay curious. Stay kind. And always look twice before you throw something away.

MINDSET RULE SIX
CELEBRATE FAILURE
DRAFT

Mindset Rule Six

Celebrate Failure

Let's be honest: failure hits adults differently. It comes with bills, reputations, resumes, and responsibilities. A failed project can feel like proof that you should have known better, tried less, or stayed safe. But avoiding failure doesn't prevent loss; it only postpones growth. The maker's mindset doesn't deny the cost of failure; it teaches you how to recover from it with dignity, insight, and momentum.

The sound of a crack in a middle school classroom can be louder than thunder. A student grips a 3D-printed part a little too tightly, and *snap*, half the room gasps. I don't. I smile. "Congratulations," I tell them. "You just learned more than half the engineers in America do in a week."

They expect me to be angry. They expect punishment, a grade drop, maybe even a disappointed sigh. But not here. In my classroom, failure isn't the end, it's the report card of real life.

Most students don't fear breaking something. They fear being seen breaking something. That fear isn't natural, it's trained. Somewhere between kindergarten and middle school, we're taught that mistakes are marks against our worth. Red ink, test grades, public corrections, they all reinforce the same message: don't risk looking wrong. Over time, our brains link failure with embarrassment and fear.

That's why the first step in learning to celebrate failure is to reframe it. We stop asking "*Who failed?*" and start asking "*What failed?*" It's not the person who's broken, it's the process. And once we fix the process, the person grows stronger.

When we stop defending our mistakes, we start analyzing them. That's when real creativity begins.

Maker's Note

Every invention worth keeping was built on top of what broke. In my classroom, I try to reprogram how students think about mistakes. I build small failures into lessons. Circuits that don't work. A missing semicolon in code. A 3D model just a hair too tall to print. We fix them together, we laugh, and the tension breaks. Students learn that mistakes don't define them, they teach them. Over time, something magical happens and failure stops being terrified. It becomes expected, normal, even celebrated. The classroom starts to feel alive. The energy shifts from fear to curiosity, and curiosity is where learning lives.

The best engineers aren't fearless. They just know how to keep working through the fear until the fear gives up. We praise finished products but never show the bruises that came before them. Every great idea, the light bulb, WD-40, Dyson vacuums, was born from thousands of wrong turns. The only reason we have them today is because someone refused to quit.

Maker's Mindset

Failure Wall

A failure wall is often needed to show others where failures occur. It's a big whiteboard covered in sticky notes. Each one lists something that went wrong and what was learned. No names, just lessons. "3D printer jammed: clean the nozzle." "LED blew out: check resistance." "Hot glue gun exploded: don't use it upside down."

By the end of the semester, the wall is full. It looks like chaos to an outsider, but it's really a map of progress. Every mistake on that board represents a student who kept going. And that's worth more than any perfect score.

Reflection Point

When students stop hiding their failures, they start learning without limits. Failure isn't an insult, it's information. It's feedback. It's the most honest data you'll ever receive. When you see failure as feedback, the fear starts to fade. The focus shifts from shame to strategy, from emotion to exploration. And suddenly, failure becomes the teacher.

So how do you build this mindset? Start small. Fail safely. Break something, burn out a bulb, mess up the code. Then laugh about it. Write down what happened and what you learned. Talk about it openly. Each time you do, your brain learns that mistakes aren't fatal, they're formative.

Learning is a loop: you try, you fail, you adjust, you try again. The only way to stop learning is to stop trying. When people freeze out of fear, the loop dies. But when we keep the loop open, by trying again, laughing again, reflecting again, we turn failure into momentum.

In my own life, I've learned this the hard way. Every failed prototype, every short circuit, every burned batch of hot sauce, each one taught me something irreplaceable. Over time, I realized that failure isn't the enemy of mastery, it's the path to it.

You don't reach mastery by avoiding errors. You reach it by recovering faster. Mastery isn't about never falling down; it's about how gracefully you stand back up.

The only failure that teaches nothing is the one you refuse to face. We've been conditioned to believe failure defines us, but it doesn't. Failure refines us. It sands off arrogance, polishes humility, and strengthens resolve. It's the forge where creativity is tempered into wisdom.

So celebrate failure. Laugh at it. Share it. Teach it. Because every time you do, you teach the next generation that learning isn't about getting it right, it's about getting better.

You can't celebrate success until you've learned to celebrate the lessons that tried to stop you. That's where the maker's mindset truly begins, not in perfection, but in persistence. And that's where the next story starts, with a bottle of hot sauce, 356 failed attempts, and the taste of what it really means to celebrate failure.

Maker's Mindset

Deep Dive 6.1: Lewis and the Peanut Butter Gun

There's a scene in Meet the Robinsons that every engineer, every teacher, and every curious kid should have framed on their wall. It's not the dramatic moment of discovery or the emotional ending. It's the peanut butter gun.

Lewis, a bright-eyed inventor with hair as wild as his imagination, decides to fix a broken gadget that flings peanut butter. Like all engineers, he believes the world can be made better, or at least more interesting, through the application of creativity and elbow grease. With excitement, he tweaks a few gears, resets a spring, and gives it a test fire.

Boom!

Peanut butter everywhere. Ceiling, walls, clothes, and pride, covered. Lewis freezes, expecting punishment, embarrassment, or maybe even laughter at his expense. But instead, the family around him erupts into cheers. Applause. Celebration. They don't mock failure, they honor it.

And that's when the movie delivers one of the most powerful maker's ever animated lessons.

Celebrating failure.

When you cheer for failure, you rewire the brain to chase progress instead of perfection. The Robinson family didn't just cheer for Lewis; they treated failure like an essential family ritual. Their entire home, every gadget, every room, is built on experimentation. There's a doorbell that barks, a hat that thinks, and a time machine that barely holds itself together. The family motto, printed and repeated with the warmth of wisdom, is simple: *Keep Moving Forward.* That phrase is more than motivation. It's a psychological reprogramming tool. Most of us are trained from early childhood to associate mistakes with shame, the red marks on our papers, the sighs from our teachers, the smirks from our peers. By the time we reach adulthood, failure has become emotional poison. We avoid it at all costs.

But the Robinsons? They've detoxed from that fear. They don't just accept failure; they celebrate it because they know the brain learns faster when it's curious and unafraid. When I show this clip in my classroom, students laugh first, then stare wide-eyed when the cheering starts. I tell them, "That right there is what a healthy maker mindset looks like. No one gets it right the first time, but everyone learns something when they try."

In a healthy system, failure isn't a dead end. It's feedback.

Reflection Point:

Failure is a family trait in every creative lineage. You don't inherit perfection, you inherit perseverance.

Later in the movie, Lewis is taken to the future where he meets Cornelius Robinson, the grown-up version of himself. There's another moment of peanut butter, but this time it's not a machine. It's lunch.

The family gathers to make "The Perfect PB&J." Except, it's anything but perfect. Peanut butter oozes out, jelly splatters, and bread tears. It's messy. Glorious. Human. And yet, they're all laughing.

That's the other half of the lesson: perfection is a myth. The future, no matter how advanced, shiny, or automated, will always include a bit of chaos. And that's not failure; that's flavor.

When we embrace imperfection, we let go of the toxic myth that success is a straight line. Creativity lives in the curves, the splatters, and the crooked sandwiches of life.

I tell my students all the time: "You'll never find innovation where fear of failure is the policy." Reflection is how a system learns without breaking itself.

Maker's Note:

The perfect PB&J doesn't exist. But the pursuit of it makes you a better cook, and a better thinker.

Psychologically speaking, what the Robinsons demonstrate is cognitive reframing. They take an event that would normally trigger embarrassment or shame and replace it with joy and curiosity. Over time, this teaches the brain to see failure not as danger but as data.

Our fear of failure comes from what's called ego threat. When something we try doesn't work, our identity feels attacked, we make a mistake with a process error for a personal flaw. The way out of that trap is to separate the two.

In my classroom, I call this the "who" versus the "what" problem. Don't ask who failed. Ask what failed.

By shifting focus to the experiment instead of the experiment, students stop defending their ego and start defending their process. That's when true learning happens, and when curiosity finally replaces fear.

Failure is not an insult to your intelligence; it's an invitation to apply it.

When I teach, my classroom looks a lot like the Robinsons' living room. Things buzz, hum, click, and occasionally burst into sparks. A soldering iron burns out. A servo locks up. Someone's 3D print looks like a plate of spaghetti. It's all part of the process.

The first reaction from students is always the same, shock, frustration, maybe a bit of laughter. But that's when I step in and say, "Congratulations. You just had your peanut butter gun moment."

They smile, but they also get it. Because by this point, we've talked about what failure really means. It's not about mistakes; it's about messages. Every misfire tells you something new.

I've seen timid students become innovators simply because I refused to let them hide from failure. I've seen kids who thought they "weren't good at engineering" turn into confident makers once they realized the room is a lab, not a test.

And every time a project goes sideways, I cheer, not sarcastically, but sincerely. Because each time they fail, they become less afraid of trying again.
Failure is contagious, but so is courage.

"Keep Moving Forward" isn't just a slogan for dreamers. It's a practical engineering rule. When something breaks, you move forward by examining, documenting, and iterating. When your design flops, you move forward by revising your assumptions. When your ego gets bruised, you move forward by remembering it is not personal, it's professional growth in disguise.

Walt Disney himself once said, "Around here, we don't look backwards for very long. We keep moving forward, opening new doors and doing new things, because we're curious. And curiosity keeps leading us down new paths."

Curiosity is the antidote to fear. It's what keeps makers from becoming critics and keeps teachers from becoming judges. The Robinsons' household is a metaphor for what every creative space should feel like: a little chaotic, a little messy, and always full of motion. The future belongs to the ones who keep building while others keep blaming.

Every generation needs its own version of the peanut butter gun, a reminder that the things we build might explode, but the explosion is part of education. Lewis thought he'd be punished. Instead, he celebrated. That single moment of emotional surprise rewrote his story. And that's exactly what happens when we stop fearing failure, we rewrite our own.

In my classroom, when something breaks, I remind students: "Setback, it is not. It's data. Write it down, learn from it, and keep moving forward." I've learned to love the smell of failure, even if it's a faint whiff of burnt wire or melted plastic, because it means something new is being tried. Learning is alive.

If success is sweet, failure is the peanut butter that sticks with you. The beauty of Meet the Robinsons isn't in its futuristic gadgets or time-travel paradoxes. It's in its fearless humanity. Lewis fails forward into his future, one peanut butter splatter at a time. When he meets his older self,

Cornelius, and sees how those messy, awkward moments led to something extraordinary, it's a message for all of us: you can't edit your way to greatness, you have to build your way there.

Every project we take on has the potential to splatter. But every splatter has the potential to teach. So, the next time your idea backfires, your prototype melts, or your project flops, remember this: The future doesn't belong to the perfect, it belongs to the persistent.

Practice random acts of kindness and thoughtless acts of beauty

MINDSET RULE SEVEN
DO YOUR BEST
THEN
DO BETTER

Mindset Rule Seven

Do Your Best, Then Do Better

If Celebrate Failure is about falling forward, then Do Your Best, Then Do Better is about what you do once you've landed.

It's the flip side of the same coin , the one that shines because it's been handled, dropped, polished, and passed through a few lessons.

This rule is simple, but it's not easy: Be your absolute personal best. Then do better.

That's it.

And that's everything.

It's not about competition with others, it's about growth against your own baseline. Because excellence isn't a trophy you win once; it's a habit you maintain forever.

The Problem with "Good Enough"

There's a quiet, dangerous phrase that stops more innovation than failure ever could: "That's good enough."

"Good enough" is a trap disguised as relief. It feels like progress, smells like success, but behaves like quicksand. You think you're done, but what you've really done is stopped moving.

As makers, teachers, and lifelong learners, we've all been there, that point where fatigue, pride, or frustration whispers, "Close enough." You test a prototype, it works once, and your brain releases a wave of satisfaction so strongly it drowns out curiosity.

Psychologically, this is called the comfort plateau. Your brain's reward system floods you with dopamine the first time something works, but it stops rewarding you for improving it. Unless you consciously push past that initial victory, you begin to stagnate.

"Good enough" is the point where growth goes to die. I call this "the Half-Assed Horizon." You can see the next level from where you're standing, but you convince yourself it's too far to walk. True mastery begins right there, in that moment when you could stop and no one would blame you, but you choose not to.

The Hot Sauce Epiphany

When I first started making hot sauce, I thought I had it all figured out. The bottles looked decent, the flavor was strong, and people said, "Hey, that's pretty good." Pretty good felt like a win, until one summer afternoon changed everything.

I had been roasting vegetables for dinner, peppers, onions, and garlic. The smell filled the kitchen like an invitation from heaven. On a whim, I tossed some roasted peppers into my next sauce batch. The result was shocking.

Smoky. Deep. Alive.

It was the same base recipe, but the difference was night and day.

That was my *do better* moment. It wasn't about adding more ingredients or chasing complexity, it was about refinement.

Maker's Mindset

Iteration.

The lesson was simple: I hadn't achieved my best. I had just reached my current best.

Maker's Note: The distance between "good" and "great" is measured in curiosity, not luck.

From then on, I approached every batch like an experiment. What happens if I toast the cumin first? What if I use smoked salt instead of regular? What if I ferment instead of boiling? Each variation was a step beyond the previous limit. Some were flops. Others were gold. But all of them moved me forward.

Doing better isn't about chasing perfection. It's about chasing understanding.

Growth Is a Decision, Not an Accident

No one stumbles into growth. You can stumble into failure, that's easy, but growth requires awareness, intention, and humility.

After every project, I now do a debrief. When something works, I ask:

Why did it work?

What conditions made it succeed?

Can I repeat it under stress?

How can I improve it by 10%, even if it already shines?

This is the reverse twin of the "Celebrate Failure" wall. That wall tracks what broke; this one track what worked. Together, they form a complete learning cycle, the engineering loop of growth.

Reflection Point:

Failure shows you what to fix. Success shows you what to refine.

I tell my students, "Write down every victory, not to brag, but to learn from it."

Documentation keeps truth alive.

Psychology of Continuous Growth

In psychology, there's something called the competence loop. It's the cycle your brain follows when learning a skill: try, fail, adjust, succeed, and repeat. The moment you stop reflecting, the loop collapses.

There's also the Dunning–Kruger effect, which describes how people who know a little tend to think they know a lot. Ironically, the more skilled you become, the more you realize how much more there is to learn.

That's why experts are humble, not because they lack confidence, but because they've seen how deep the well goes.

Maker's Note: Confidence is knowing you can do it again, not pretending you've done it perfectly.

The trick is to treat every success like a checkpoint, not a finish line. Each win is a data point, a snapshot of what worked at that time, under those conditions. But time changes. Tools change. You change. So, your process must evolve, too.

The Standard You Set

Every classroom, workshop, and studio has an invisible temperature, the standard the leader sets. If I settle for mediocrity, my

Maker's Mindset

students will too. If I demand improvement, not perfection, but improvement, they rise to meet it.

I once told a class of budding engineers: "Your best is today's measurement. Tomorrow, I expect a new one." That wasn't pressure, it was permission. Permission to grow, to explore, to redefine themselves. I've seen it happen time and again: a student who once celebrated a blinking LED later refines the circuit until it becomes a functioning robot. The same kid who once said, "It works!" later says, "It works, but it could work better." That's the moment I live for, when curiosity surpasses compliance.

Reflection Point: Doing your best once is performance. Doing better every time after is character.

The Mirror of Mindset Rule #6

If Rule #6, Celebrate Failure, teaches resilience, then Rule #7 teaches evolution. The two aren't opposites, they're partners. You learn by failing, and then you grow by improving what succeeded. One without the other creates imbalance: If you only celebrate failure, you risk never advancing. If you only demand improvement, you risk burning out. Together, they form a rhythm, fall, rise, refine, repeat. That's the true maker's heartbeat. You can't celebrate progress if you never pause to measure it.

How to Practice "Do Better"

Here's a simple system you can use, the Maker's Loop for Growth:

1. Reflect: After each project, write what worked and why.

2. Refine: Identify one aspect to improve (design, efficiency, clarity, etc.).

3. Rebuild: Apply that improvement intentionally.

4. Repeat: Start again.

That's it. Simple, but transformative.

It's the same principle behind Kaizen, the Japanese philosophy of small, continuous improvement. It's not about massive leaps but micro-adjustments. One percent better each day.

If you improve by one percent daily, you'll be 37 times better by the end of the year. (Math doesn't lie, compounding growth works.)

Reflection Point

The habit of improvement compounds faster than the habit of excuses.

The "Better" Mindset in Practice

When my students build something that finally works, I can almost see their dopamine spike. Their faces light up, shoulders relax, and pride kicks in. I let them enjoy that moment, then I strike.

"Now," I say, "how could it work better?" The first reaction is usually disbelief. Better? It works! But once they start thinking about it, something beautiful happens, they begin noticing small imperfections they'd ignored before. Wobbly joints. Wires too long. Design inefficiencies. They start refining instead of repeating. That's when they stop being students and start becoming engineers.

Maker's Mindset

You Can't Outgrow Curiosity

The day you think you've reached your peak is the day you start slipping backward. Growth isn't a mountain you climb once; it's a treadmill that moves under your feet. If you stop walking, it pulls you back.

Curiosity is your engine. Reflection is your steering. Humility is your fuel.

Maker's Note: The world doesn't reward potential, it rewards persistence.

Final Reflection

Doing your best is not about exhausting yourself. It's about engaging yourself. It's not about perfection; it's about progression. Each time you build, code, teach, or design, ask yourself, "What worked? Why did it work? And how can I make it better?"

Because that's how greatness happens. Not overnight. Not in leaps. But in small, deliberate, curious steps. The maker's journey is a conversation between who you are and who you're becoming.

Rule #6 tells you not to fear mistakes.

Rule #7 tells you not to fear success either, because even that can be improved upon.

Your best is the beginning of your next.

Deep Dive 7.1: The Student Who Did Better

Every year I meet a handful of students who remind me why I teach. One in particular stand out, a seventh grader who struggled through her first design project. Her robot didn't move, her code didn't compile, and her frustration boiled just below the surface. When I asked what she thought went wrong, she said, 'Everything.' I smiled and told her, 'Good. Now you know what not to do.'

She didn't like that answer, but she took it seriously. The next week she came in with a completely new design, no glitter, no color, just wires, code, and determination. Her second attempt worked flawlessly. When I asked what changed, she said, 'I just wanted to see if I could do better.' That's it. That's the entire point of this rule. Improvement is not born from success; it grows from dissatisfaction with 'good enough.'

By the time the semester ended, she wasn't just improving her projects; she was improving her mindset. She learned to take pride not in finishing, but in refining. That's how real makers grow, one reflection, one iteration, one quiet victory at a time.

Maker's Note: Real progress happens in the rework, not the result.

Deep Dive 7.2: Curiosity with Hot Sauces

When I first started making hot sauces, I thought the goal was heat. The hotter the better, right? Wrong. What I learned through dozens of failed batches, too smoky, too acidic, too bland, was that balance mattered far more than intensity. Each failure forced me to adjust ratios, try new peppers, change how I roasted or smoked the ingredients. Over time, 'Recipe #357' became a favorite not because it was perfect, but because it had history, the fingerprints of 356 failures behind it.

That's what this rule means. Do your best with what you know, what you have, and who you are, and then do better, because your next version will always know more than your last. Makers who stop improving stop being makers. Perfection is not the destination. Refinement is the practice.

Reflection Point: The best version of your work will always be the next one.

Deep Dive 7.3: The Psychology of Growth

Psychologically, our brains crave comfort. Once we achieve competence, dopamine rewards us, signaling that we've 'made it.' This reward loop can become a trap, a plateau of complacency. To grow beyond that, we must consciously seek discomfort, retrain our thinking, and view challenge as opportunity.

Ego and fear of failure both resist this change. Ego whispers, 'You're already the best.' Fear whispers, 'What if I can't do better?' The truth is that growth happens precisely when ego and fear collide, and we choose to push forward anyway.

In the classroom, this means embracing feedback, experimenting without shame, and learning to love revision.

Maker's Note: Growth is uncomfortable because comfort never makes anything grow.

Final Reflection

Do your best, then do better. It's simple, but it's not easy. This rule is the reason champions go back to the gym after winning, and why great inventors revisit their blueprints long after a product succeeds. Growth is not about what others expect of you, it's about who you choose to become next.

In every project, ask yourself: 'Is this my best work?' If the answer is yes, then smile, because tomorrow, that answer should be no. There is always another layer of improvement waiting for those brave enough to look for it.

Maker's Mindset

When we teach our students, peers, or children to celebrate this mindset, we don't just teach them how to make things, we teach them how to become better humans. Every design, every plan, every lesson learned becomes a step toward their next best version.

Stay curious. Stay humble. And always, do better.

MINDSET RULE EIGHT
SHARE

Mindset Rule Eight

Share

"Ideas only live when they move."

The Spark You Can't Keep

It started with a screw. A brass screw rolled across the classroom floor and vanished beneath a row of lockers. The moment it disappeared, a sixth grader named Riley froze mid-sentence, staring at the spot like it had swallowed her future. That single screw held together the left arm of her cardboard robot; a project she had poured every lunch period into.

Without it, the robot's elbow sagged like a tired soldier. Riley sighed. "Well... I guess that's it.

Across the room, another student rummaging through a toolbox overheard her. He held up a small jar.

"I've got extras." He said to her, holding the jar up like a trophy.

Riley blinked. "Really?"

"Yeah. Take one. I found them in the scrap bin."

Two minutes later, the robot stood upright again, waving its arm stiffly as if saluting the idea of cooperation itself. The classroom erupted in laughter and applause, and Riley shouted, "Thank you!" with genuine joy.

That moment, small, ordinary, almost forgettable, was the seed of this rule. Every great innovation, every leap of progress, every moment of grace in human history starts with a choice like that: to share instead of withholding.

The Paradox of Possession

The strange thing about ideas is that we think they're fragile, like bubbles that might pop if anyone else touches them. In truth, ideas are closer to fire, beautiful when tended, destructive when hoarded. When early humans discovered how to make fire, it wasn't one person's secret; it was a gift to the tribe. When they shared that gift, they unlocked warmth, protection, and civilization itself.

But somewhere along the road to modernity, we began treating ideas like property deeds instead of campfires. We began to measure ownership rather than impact.

"I had that idea first."

"I don't want anyone stealing it."

"I'll share after I'm done."

In every workshop, every classroom, every company boardroom, those same thoughts echo in different forms. And each time we silence an idea out of fear, the world grows a little dimmer.

Here's the paradox: the moment you give an idea away is the moment it begins to grow. Knowledge doesn't diminish when shared, it multiplies. The more you offer, the more you receive in return. In the maker world, we do not call this poetry; We call it physics. Circuits complete only when connected. Knowledge behaves the same way.

Maker's Mindset

Physics of Sharing

When you pass an idea to someone else, you're not losing it, you're creating resonance. Like two tuning forks vibrating in harmony, shared understanding amplifies both minds. That's why good teachers don't hoard techniques; they spread them. That's why open-source programmers publish code freely, knowing others will improve it. That's why the greatest inventions, from Faraday's dynamo to Tesla's wireless current, came not from isolation, but from communities of thinkers pushing one another forward.

In my classroom, the energy is palpable when students start swapping solutions. You can feel the hum of shared learning, a kind of creative current that travels faster than any Wi-Fi signal. Some call it collaboration. I call it human circuitry.

Why We Hide

If sharing is so powerful, why do we struggle with it? Because fear, ego, and greed are brilliant liars.

Fear whispers: *"They'll steal your work."*

Ego hisses: *"You don't need their help."*

Greed smiles: *"You can profit if you keep it to yourself."*

Those three voices have sabotaged more progress than failure ever could. They build invisible walls around creativity and convince us that isolation is safety. But safety is the opposite of growth. In the workshop of life, rust forms on anything that sits unused. Knowledge, compassion, skill, if you don't circulate them, they corrode. The truth is that sharing is not naïve; it's courageous. It requires vulnerability and trust. It's standing in the open saying, "Here's what I've made, what do you see that I don't?"

The Evolution of Collaboration

Sharing isn't a new idea; it's humanity's oldest operating system. Long before patents, trade secrets, or social media, knowledge spread through stories. Hunters taught younger hunters how to track. Midwives passed healing wisdom from mother to daughter. Sailors traded star maps in smoky taverns. Every generation built its foundation on the generosity of the one before. Somewhere in that timeline, we traded oral tradition for competition. But the essence never vanished, it just went digital.

The open-source revolution revived the ancient practice of shared creation. When engineers upload schematics or educators publish lesson plans freely, they're echoing the oldest human instinct: to build together. The first 3D-printed prosthetic hands, the Raspberry Pi community, even global humanitarian drone networks, none of these exist without collaboration. When we share ideas, we're not just creating objects. We're creating lineage.

The Workshop as a Microcosm

My classroom is a living experiment in shared progress. We start each semester with a single rule written in large letters on the whiteboard: "No idea belongs to one person once it's spoken." It's not about ownership; it's about momentum. When a student suggests a way to fix a servo problem, others test it, remix it, and improve it. By the end, the original idea has evolved far beyond its creator's intent. Instead of resentment, there's pride.

"Hey, that's my design in there!"

"Yeah but look what we added!"

You can't teach that kind of collaboration from a textbook. You teach it by letting go. Once students experience how sharing accelerates progress, they start applying it everywhere, coding groups, art projects, even homework. The classroom becomes a network of nodes, each pulsing with creativity that feeds the others.

The Cost of Secrecy

I once had a colleague who refused to share her project lesson plans. She believed they gave her an edge; proof she was the most creative teacher on the team. She guarded her materials like state secrets. When she left the school, her hard drive was erased. Years of innovation vanished overnight. No legacy, no collaboration, no continuity, just digital dust. Contrast that with another teacher who uploaded her designs to a shared drive accessible to every instructor in the district. Her projects spread across campuses, inspiring new iterations she never dreamed of. Years later, teachers still mention her work in training. That's the real difference: hoarded knowledge dies with you. Shared knowledge outlives you.

The Emotional Currency of Generosity

There's an emotional alchemy that happens when you give without expecting anything back. You begin to feel lighter, more connected, more alive.

Sharing doesn't just benefit others, it reshapes you. It replaces scarcity with abundance, loneliness with belonging.

Every time I share a lesson plan, a design file, or even a failed prototype, I'm reminded that generosity is a form of engineering. It reroutes the circuits of the heart to power something larger than self-interest.

The Classroom Network Effect

When teachers share, students thrive. When students share, the classroom transforms. I once assigned my seventh graders a group challenge: design a small bridge from popsicle sticks that could hold ten pounds. Each group tested, failed, and adjusted. But the real magic happened during open lab days, when teams started wandering at each other's tables, comparing methods. Within hours, the room sounded like a marketplace of ideas:

"Try layering your trusses."

"We switched glue types, it made a difference."

"Use triangles, not squares!"

By the final day, every bridge held. Not because each group perfected their own design, but because they shared what worked and what didn't. That's the network effect in action, an ecosystem of minds cross-pollinating toward collective success.

Sharing in the Age of Noise

Let's be honest, modern life doesn't make sharing easy. Social media turned the act of sharing into performance. Likes replaced dialogue.

Maker's Mindset

Posts replaced conversation. We confuse broadcasting with connecting. Real sharing is slower and riskier. It happens in coffee shops, classrooms, and late-night message threads when people care enough to help each other grow. It's the kind that listens more than it speaks. You don't need a viral post to make a difference. You just need one person willing to listen, build, and pass it forward.

The Maker's Code

There's a quiet code among true makers, a set of unspoken ethics that separate the opportunists from the builders of communities. Credit generously. Names are free; give them away. Teach what you've learned, not just what you've built. Never hoard information that could help someone grow. If someone improves their idea, celebrate, not compete. When in doubt, ask: would the world be better if I shared this? These aren't rules of etiquette, they're blueprints for legacy.

The Gift of Shared Failure

Some of the most valuable things I've ever shared weren't successes, they were mistakes. Students learn more from seeing a failed prototype than a perfect one. Colleagues learn more from hearing how a project broke than how it worked.

Failure becomes fertilizer when it's shared. It feeds the next generation of makers and reminds them that progress is messy, not miraculous.

When people see you openly admitting your mistakes, they stop fearing themselves. And in that moment, you become more than a maker, you become a mentor.

The Reciprocity of Teaching

Every time I explain a concept, I end up understanding it better. Teaching is the purest form of sharing because it loops back into self-growth. One of my favorite phrases is, "The master is just the student who never stopped explaining." That's how communities evolve, each generation explaining what they know until the next surpasses them. True educators don't build monuments; they build bridges.

Sharing Across Generations

When I was in the Navy, I learned a lesson that stuck with me longer than any technical manual. On the ship, knowledge wasn't stored in databases, it was passed down. Old sailors taught the younger ones through stories, rituals, and habits. They didn't guard wisdom; they gifted it, because someone once did the same for them. That cycle of mentorship is how institutions survive storms, literal and metaphorical. It's how humans ensure that no generation starts from zero.

The same applies in every classroom, every lab, every household. Share what you know, and you turn experience into legacy.

When Sharing Hurts

Not every act of generosity is met with gratitude. Sometimes, people take credit for your work. Sometimes, your openness is mistaken for weakness. Sometimes, the world rewards selfishness louder than kindness. Share anyway.

Because the moment you stop giving, you stop growing. Your ideas, like seeds, might fall on rocky ground, but some will land in fertile soil. And even if one person misuses your trust, ten others will use your gift to build something better.

The alternative, silence, isolation, creative stinginess, is far worse.

Deep Dive 8.1: The Story of Two Engineers

Years ago, two engineers approached a similar problem: designing a compact, efficient electric motor. One guarded his notes like classified documents. The other published his designs online, inviting feedback. Within months, the second engineer's design outperformed the first, not because he was smarter, but because he had an army of unseen collaborators refining his work.

When asked why he shared so freely, he said, "I'd rather be part of the conversation that changes the world than the patent that's forgotten." That's the spirit of this rule.

The Fire That Never Fades

Remember the metaphor of fire? A single flame can light thousands of candles without losing its glow. That's what happens when you share, whether it's a piece of knowledge, a resource, or a simple act of encouragement. The light spreads, the warmth grows, and the darkness retreats a little more.

If the Maker's Mindset has a heartbeat, it's this: we rise by building together.

So, share your tools. Share your notes. Share your time.

Because the universe itself runs on shared energy, and every spark you give returns tenfold in light.

Maker's Takeaway

"Knowledge is the only resource that multiplies when divided.

A true maker doesn't just build things, they build others."

Maker's Mindset

Deep Dive 8.2: The Coffee Shop Laboratory

Where shared ideas blow stronger than espresso.

The Unplanned Workshop

If you want to understand how innovation happens, skip the corporate boardroom and spend an afternoon in a coffee shop. Not the kind with everyone glued to a laptop and noise-canceling headphones, the other kind. The messy, noisy, charming ones where people still talk to strangers. That's where you'll find the unofficial laboratories of the modern world. Ideas don't just hatch there, they bump into each other, cross-pollinate, and evolve over half-finished lattes.

Some of the most profound projects of my teaching career began not at a conference or professional development session, but at a small table in a corner café surrounded by mismatched chairs and the aroma of roasted beans.

I used to grade papers there. Then one day, a fellow teacher from another district asked what I was working on. I told her about a new robotics lesson. She leaned forward. "Mind if I see?" Twenty minutes later, we had redesigned half the project together. By the end of the week, she'd tested it with her students, improved it, and sent the results back to me. That simple exchange, two teachers, one napkin, and a cappuccino, has since evolved into a shared open curriculum used by dozens of classrooms.

No contracts. No meetings. Just conversation.

The Geometry of Tables

Every table in a coffee shop is a geometry of collaboration waiting to happen. Rectangular tables divide space: mine versus yours. Round tables invite sharing. There's no head, no hierarchy, just flow. I learned to bring extra notepads and markers because people nearby would inevitably join in.

"What are you sketching?" Asks one of my unofficial cohorts.

"An Arduino project."

"Oh, I'm a designer! Want to see how I'd wire it differently?"

And there it begins: the spontaneous, caffeine-powered brainstorming that has probably generated more innovation per square foot than some billion-dollar offices. That's the hidden truth about creativity; it thrives where formality doesn't. A napkin, a doodle, a laugh, that's the architecture of sharing.

The Coffee Shop as Ecosystem

Every regular café has its ecosystem of creators:

The writer who uses the same seat every morning.

The student grinding through calculus homework.

The barista studying graphic design on break.

The retiree who reads the paper and dispenses wisdom between refills.

At first glance, their separate planets orbit the same sun. But once conversation starts, gravity takes over. The writer asks the designer about layouts. The retiree tells a story that becomes the writer's next plot twist.

Maker's Mindset

The student offers to proofread. It's a quiet miracle of mutual uplift. No one's officially teaching, yet everyone's learning.

That's what happens when people share space and curiosity. It's what every good classroom tries to replicate, a safe, low-stakes environment where ideas can wander without judgment.

Makers Without Badges

One of my favorite memories happened on a rainy Saturday. I was sketching a low-cost sensor rig for a student weather project when an older gentleman sat beside me. He looked over and said, "That's not a bad circuit, but your resistor's off by about 20 ohms."

I blinked. "You're an engineer?"

He smiled. "Retired. But habits die hard."

Two hours later, we redesigned the circuit together. He shared stories of troubleshooting Apollo guidance computers. I told him how seventh graders get excited when LEDs blink. We traded email addresses. A week later, he visited my classroom as a guest volunteer.

The students called him Mr. Rocket Man. He called them colleagues.

None of it would have happened if either of us had been too proud, or too shy, to share a table. That's the point: you never know who's sitting next to you. Every stranger carries a library of expertise waiting to be opened.

The Myth of Isolation

Society romanticizes the "lone genius", the inventor in the garage, the artist in the attic, the coder in a dark room. But history tells a different story.

Edison had a team of twenty machinists. Da Vinci apprenticed with Verrocchio.

Steve Jobs didn't design alone; he sparked and collided with Wozniak, Hertzfeld, and dozens of others. Isolation breeds originality only in myth. Collaboration is the actual engine of progress. Even the greatest minds used coffeehouse conversations to shape revolutions, literally. In 17th-century London, coffeehouses were nicknamed "penny universities." You could buy a cup, join a debate, and leave with a better education than most classrooms could offer.

Newton, Hooke, and Halley traded experiments there. The stock exchange, insurance industry, and even scientific peer review were born over those wooden counters.

Today's coffee shops are their spiritual descendants. They remind us that humanity's best ideas rarely begin in silence.

The Two-Dollar Whiteboard

During one particularly stormy week, our school's makerspace lost power. No computers, no soldering irons, nothing but flashlights and chalk.

Rather than cancel, I took my students to a nearby café that had backup generators and free Wi-Fi. I bought everyone hot chocolate, commandeered a wall, and taped up a sheet of butcher paper. "Okay," I said. "This is our new whiteboard. Let's share one idea each for a project that doesn't need electricity."

Maker's Mindset

They filled the wall with sketches, mechanical wind toys, marble mazes, and paper automata. Customers started watching. Then a woman approached and said, "I teach art at the high school. Mind if I add something?" Within an hour, our "coffee shop lab" had grown into an impromptu community event. Customers shared materials, ideas, and stories. The café owner offered to host future sessions.

That two-dollar roll of paper became a reminder that the spirit of sharing doesn't require fancy tools, just space, people, and permission to dream out loud.

The Art of Listening

Sharing isn't just speaking; it's listening with intent. In those informal labs, you learn the rhythm of true collaboration: talk less, absorb more, and notice what excites people.

Once, a student joined one of our off-campus sessions and barely spoke the whole time. At the end, she shyly showed a sketch of a kinetic sculpture she'd been working on at home. It used nothing but recycled plastic bottles and string, yet it was mesmerizing, a dancing column of light and shadow. The group fell silent. Then applause broke out. That quiet moment taught more about the power of shared encouragement than any rubric ever could.

Some people bloom only when the room listens first.

The Currency of Coffee

Why do ideas flow more freely over coffee than in meetings? Because coffee shops operate on trust and ritual rather than authority. No one needs permission to speak. No agenda to follow. No minutes to record. The only currency is curiosity. You pay attention, not approval. When people feel safe to share without fear of looking foolish, creativity skyrockets.

Teachers can replicate this magic by designing "idea cafés" in classrooms, weekly open sessions where students discuss their projects informally, swap feedback, and build on each other's insights. It's remarkable how many breakthroughs happen when grades aren't on the line.

When Sharing Becomes Contagious

After years of holding these informal sessions, something surprising happened. Students began hosting their own outside of class. One Saturday, I found a group of them at a local café, laptops open, building an Arduino-based light show. They called it "*Makers on the Move.* They weren't competing for credit or grades; they were helping each other. One student said, "We figured if you (the professor) can share ideas over coffee, we can too."

This provided me with validation for stating that sharing isn't taught, it's modeled. When people witness generosity, they imitate it. When they experience trust, they extend it. The ripple effect of one open conversation can reach far beyond the original circle.

Beyond the Mug

Of course, not every coffee shop conversation leads to a masterpiece. Some end with spilled drinks, dead ends, or terrible puns. But even those moments have value because they strengthen connection, the invisible infrastructure of collaboration. Makerspaces and classrooms thrive not on perfect ideas, but on the willingness to keep talking, sketching, and laughing together. That's the "laboratory" part, not experiments with chemicals, but with conversation itself.

Every interaction is a small test: what happens if we combine this perspective with that one? What if we add humor? What if we stir in empathy?
Sometimes the results fizz, sometimes they flop, but every test builds understanding.

A coffee shop isn't just a place, it's a mindset. When we choose to sit together, we create the conditions for collaboration. When we share freely, we become catalysts for others. The world doesn't need more geniuses guarding secrets. It needs more tables, more laughter, more napkin sketches. Because every great invention, movement, and friendship began the same way, with someone saying, *"Mind if I sit here?"*

Deep Dive 8.3: The Gift Economy of Ideas

Every economy is built on exchange. Some trade in money, some in time, some in trust. But the most powerful economy, the one that fuels progress, innovation, and even happiness, is the gift economy of ideas. In this economy, the act of giving isn't charity; it's investment. Every shared insight, technique, or blueprint adds value to a collective reservoir that everyone can draw from. The more we contribute, the richer that reservoir becomes.

It's not a new concept. Ancient communities thrived on it. Villages once survived winters because neighbors shared food, fire, and skill. Guilds of craftsmen taught apprentices not out of obligation, but pride. Scientists published findings so others could build upon them. The word "colleague" literally means "one who shares labor."

Yet somewhere along the way, modern culture turned generosity into risk.

"Protect your intellectual property."

"Don't give away your secrets."

"Monetize your expertise."

And yes, protecting originality matters. But when the obsession with ownership outweighs the instinct to collaborate, creativity suffocates. You can't patent inspiration, and you can't monetize wonder without first nurturing it in others.

Maker's Mindset

The Equation of Abundance

I often tell my students, "*An idea is only valuable when it escapes your head.*" Keeping it locked away is like hiding a battery in a drawer and wondering why nothing powers on. Here's the strange math of the gift economy:

Share one idea, gain two.

Teach one skill, master it yourself.

Give one resource, receive reputation, gratitude, and insight in return.

Unlike financial economies, this one expands exponentially. The more you give, the more it grows.

A young maker once showed me a 3D-printed prosthetic hand she'd designed from open-source blueprints. "I just changed the thumb joint," she said proudly. Her improvement was shared online, where another designer saw it and refined the wrist mechanism. Within months, that collective evolution resulted in a cheaper, lighter, more functional prosthetic distributed freely to children across the world.

None of those individuals profited financially. Yet each gained something priceless: contribution, recognition, and purpose. That's the purest form of wealth.

The Psychology of Sharing

Why do some people hoard ideas while others give freely? Psychologists point to two opposing mental models: scarcity and abundance. A scarce mindset whispers: There's not enough for everyone.

If I share, I lose. An abundance mindset insists: The more I give, the more possibilities appear. In classrooms, you can see this dynamic in real time. A student afraid to share an idea during group work fears ridicule or theft. But the moment they do, when they risk being open, the group energy changes. Other students lean in, build on it, and soon that single spark becomes a collective fire.

The gift economy of ideas depends on that bravery, the willingness to trust that giving away your best thought doesn't make you poorer. It makes you part of something bigger.

The Open-Source Renaissance

In the early 1990s, a quiet rebellion reshaped technology. Programmers began rejecting the secrecy of proprietary software and started posting their code freely online. Their goal wasn't profit; it was progress. From that rebellion came Linux, Python, Arduino, and the entire maker revolution that drives classrooms like mine today. Think about that: entire industries, new careers, even this very text exist because someone decided to share what they could have locked away.

The open-source movement proved that transparency could compete with corporate control and often win. It created a new model for innovation, one built not on secrecy, but on stewardship. When a student downloads a free coding library to make a robot dance, they're not just using software. They're standing on a mountain of shared labor built by thousands of invisible teachers.

That's the beauty of open knowledge: it makes strangers into collaborators.

Maker's Mindset

The Broken Drone

A few years ago, a student named Omar brought in a busted quadcopter. The propellers were warped, the battery dead, and the controller missing.

"I found it in the trash," he said. "Can we fix it?" We disassembled it piece by piece. Most teachers would've tossed it, no budget, no parts. But then I remembered a group of online hobbyists who shared drone schematics and troubleshooting guides for free. We followed their instructions, posted photos of our progress, and even asked for help. Within a week, we had replies from around the world, people sending suggestions, links, and even a donated battery from a retired engineer in Michigan.

When we finally got the drone airborne, the entire class cheered. Omar stood there, eyes wide, as his "trash" took flight. Later, we uploaded our final modifications back to the same community. Weeks after that, someone commented, "Thanks for your guide, we used it to help kids in Peru build theirs."

That's the gift economy in action: one classroom's curiosity igniting possibilities halfway around the world.

Trust as Currency

The gift economy doesn't function without trust. You have to believe others will respect your contribution, build on it, and pay it forward. But trust doesn't mean naïveté, it means wisely generous. It's okay to watermark your work, license your code, or require credit. Transparency and acknowledgment are part of healthy ecosystems.

What's toxic is paranoia, the belief that every collaborator is a thief-in-waiting. That attitude isolates creators and kills collaboration before it begins.

I once heard a sculptor say, "You can't steal my style, you can only join it." That's wisdom. When we share freely, we stop fearing imitation and start inspiring innovation.

Gifts Create Responsibility

There's an old maker's proverb: "If you borrow knowledge, return it better." Sharing isn't an excuse for laziness; it's a call to stewardship. When someone hands you an idea, you inherit both opportunity and responsibility, to test it, refine it, and, when possible, improve it for the next person. This applies especially in teaching. Every time we adapt a colleague's lesson plan or download a resource, we borrow from that collective reservoir. The ethical move is to return something in exchange: better documentation, updated examples, or simply a thank-you note acknowledging the source.

Generosity is reciprocal. It's not about tallying debts; it's about keeping the current moving.

The Economics of Encouragement

You can measure generosity not by how much you give, but by how easily others feel empowered to give after you. Encouragement is the smallest gift with the biggest ROI. A single sentence, "That's a great idea;

you should share it!", can transform a hesitant student into a confident contributor. I've seen this countless times. A shy maker posts a prototype online expecting ridicule. Instead, someone comments, "Incredible concept, here's how you could make it even better." Suddenly, the creator is back at work, energized. That's the power of shared positivity; it compounds faster than interest.

Every act of encouragement generates more creativity than it consumes.

When Companies Forget

Corporations once learned this lesson the hard way. In the early 2000s, a major tech firm tried to crush open-source competition by locking its hardware behind proprietary code. The open-source community responded by collaborating globally, designing a compatible system from scratch, faster, cheaper, better. The company eventually pivoted, releasing its own open tools and winning back developers' respect. The irony? Their most profitable era began after they started sharing. That's because sharing builds ecosystems, and ecosystems build resilience. When you nurture a community instead of a monopoly, your influence grows long after your product fades.

Systems grow stronger when knowledge moves freely instead of being guarded.

The Classroom as a Gift Economy

My classroom runs like a small village of barterers. One student trades programming help for soldering tips. Another shares CAD designs in exchange for debugging assistance. I rarely intervene because this microeconomy teaches more than any lecture. It shows students that knowledge is not a limited commodity, it's a renewable resource sustained by collaboration. At the end of each semester, I ask them to reflect on what they gave rather than what they learned. Their answers are telling:

"I taught Maya how to use Fusion 360."

"I helped fix two robots that weren't mine."

"I shared my battery pack when someone forgot theirs."

That's when I know they've internalized the real lesson: making isn't about possession, it's about participation.

The Ego Tax

There's one cost to share that no one talks about: humility. It hurts a little to see someone improve your work. It bruises the ego to admit that others can build faster, cleaner, or smarter than you. But that's also where growth happens. The ego tax is the price of evolution. Pay it gladly. When you let go of perfectionism and embrace contribution, you graduate from "creator" to "collaborator." You stop protecting your sandbox and start expanding the playground.

The Ripple You'll Never See

Here's the quiet truth about giving ideas away: you'll never fully know where they go. That blog post, that classroom tip, that design file, each might spark a chain reaction invisible to you.

Maybe a student uses your method to invent something revolutionary ten years later. Maybe your open-source design inspires a teacher across the world to start her own program. Maybe your shared failure saves someone else from repeating it. The reward isn't fame. It's knowing that the world moves forward a fraction of an inch because you loosen your grip.

The Unfinished Blueprint

During the pandemic, I uploaded an unfinished Arduino project online, a motion-sensing hallway sanitizer dispenser I hadn't quite perfected. My code was messy, my writing inconsistent, but I thought maybe someone else could finish it.

A few months later, I received an email from a teacher in South Africa. Her students had used my design as a template and built an improved version that worked flawlessly. She attached photos of her class smiling behind masks and thumbs up. The profound notion was that I didn't lose anything by sharing an imperfect design. I gained impact I could never have achieved alone. Perfection is overrated. Contribution isn't.

The most valuable thing you can own is what you've already given away. When we treat ideas like gifts instead of currency, we build communities instead of empires. We trade ego for legacy, scarcity for abundance.

The real wealth of the maker world isn't in patents or profits, it's in participation. Every blueprint shared, every story told, every lesson posted freely becomes another spark in the collective bonfire of human creativity. Keep feeding the fire. It burns brighter when everyone adds a log.

Deep Dive 8.4: Networked Classrooms

Learning multiplies when knowledge travels freely.

The Myth of the Single Teacher

For centuries, education was built on a simple image: one teacher, one classroom, one group of students. Knowledge flowed in a single direction, chalk to board, board to notebook, notebook to test. But that model belongs to a slower age. The world now changes faster than any curriculum committee can approve. A single mind, no matter how skilled, can't keep pace with the speed of modern discovery.

Today's most powerful classrooms are networks, living systems of shared insight where teachers, students, and entire communities exchange what they know as fluidly as data through fiber optics.

A networked classroom is not a room at all. It's a state of connection.

When Teachers Teach Each Other

The best professional development I've ever experienced didn't happen at a conference. It happened in a hallway. One afternoon, while I was balancing a box of robotics kits, another teacher stopped me. "You're the guy doing the servo arm project, right? Can I steal that?"

"Only if you improve it," I said. A week later, she'd redesigned the lesson for younger students and shared her version back to me, simpler, cleaner, better documented. I started using her version. That moment revealed the secret heartbeat of modern education: collaboration isn't theft; it's refinement.

Every teacher who shares strengthens the entire system. When schools operate as closed islands, progress stagnates. But when educators connect, through shared drives, social media groups, or cross-campus visits, the tide rises for everyone.

The Ecosystem Effect

Picture a coral reef. Every organism, from the smallest polyps to the largest fish, contributes to the health of the whole. Remove collaboration, and the reef bleaches. Classrooms work the same way. Students who share ideas sustain creativity. Teachers who share methods sustain excellence. Administrators who share credit sustain morale.

A networked ecosystem doesn't just exchange information, it exchanges energy. One teacher's innovation becomes another's inspiration. One student's success becomes the model for others. When that happens, the school stops being a building and becomes a living organism that breathes progress.

The Bridge that Taught a District

In the Fall of 2018, my students built a small popsicle-stick bridge strong enough to hold forty pounds. I posted a short video on a teacher forum, mostly for fun.

Within days, I received messages from educators in three different states asking for instructions. We turned the process into a shared Google folder, photos, rubrics, test data, and reflection notes. Months later, I stumbled on a post from a school in Arizona proudly showing their bridges, crediting my class for the idea.

Then another appeared, from Canada, with improvements to the testing rig. Our humble bridge project had become a cross-continental lesson plan, refined and reimagined by dozens of teachers and hundreds of students.

That's what networked learning looks like: a single spark that becomes a constellation.

Students as Signal Boosters

The most beautiful part of this ecosystem is that students naturally continue the signal. They don't just absorb knowledge, they retransmit it. One semester, I introduced a peer-mentor program called Tech Buddies. Advanced students taught newcomers how to solder, code, and document projects. What started as a logistical fix turned into a cultural shift. When a seventh grader explained a sensor circuit better than I ever could, I felt a surge of pride as he had reached critical mass. Learning was no longer teacher-centered, it was community-centered. That's the goal of a networked classroom: to make yourself exponentially replaceable. The more you share, the less the system depends on you alone, and the stronger it becomes.

The Power of Transparency

Transparency is the fiber-optic cable of education. When teachers make their process visible, lesson plans, mistakes, iterations, they create an archive others can learn from.

During the remote learning fiasco of 2020, I started recording short "maker diaries," informal videos of daily experiments. They weren't polished. I spilled coffee, mis-wired sensors, and occasionally muttered at 3D printers.

But something unexpected happened: students began posting their own maker diaries. Then parents joined in, sharing mini projects from home. The transparency loop turned isolation into connection.

Authenticity travels faster than perfection.

Digital Villages

The Internet is often blamed for isolating people, but in the world of education, it can build villages faster than any postal system ever could. Online communities like the Arduino forums, Edmodo groups, or Reddit's r/Teachers become modern staff lounges, minus the burned coffee and budget complaints. Teachers swap ideas across continents before their morning bell even rings.

I once uploaded a simple worksheet about brainstorming through failure. By week's end, it had been translated into Spanish, Vietnamese, and Arabic by teachers I'd never met. That's not virality, it's humanity on broadband.

The Legacy Loop

The great paradox of teaching is that the more you give away, the more you endure. A teacher who hoards their materials may preserve originality, but not legacy. By contrast, a teacher who shares multiplies their influence across time zones and generations.

One of my earliest mentors, Ms. Ellis, kept a three-inch binder of her favorite projects. Before retiring, she photocopied every page and left it in the staff room with a sticky note: "Take what you need. Add what you can." Years later, I still see that binder, fatter now, edges worn, new tabs added by people she's never met.

That's immortality through generosity.

The Danger of Bandwidth Overload

Of course, networks can clog. Too much sharing without curation turns knowledge into noise. Not every idea belongs to every classroom, and not every platform deserves your time. Healthy ecosystems require filtration, mentors, moderators, and metadata. That's why reflective practice matters. Before posting or adopting a resource, ask:

Does this align with our values?

Does it enhance understanding, or just add complexity?

Will it help someone else grow, or only showcase my work?

Sharing with intention keeps the signal clean.

Cross-Pollination in Action

I once invited an art teacher to collaborate on a robotics unit. At first, she laughed. "I don't speak circuit board."

My response: "Good, teach them color theory instead."

The result was extraordinary. Students built robots that painted. They explored rhythm, symmetry, and motion through color. The art class gained engineering insight; the engineering class gained aesthetic soul.

That's the magic of cross-pollination: two worlds sharing until the boundary dissolves.

Maker's Mindset

The Student Who Reversed the Flow

During a district STEM fair, a student named Hannah stopped by my booth. She said quietly, "You don't know me, but I used your noise-meter code from your class blog." She had modified it to measure decibels during choir practice to help her classmates control volume. She showed me her version, sleeker, annotated, and completely rewritten. The teacher-student dynamic flipped. She had become the node passing knowledge back to me.

In a true network, there's no top or bottom, just flow.

The Ethics of Attribution

Networks thrive on respect. Credit is the handshake of digital collaboration. Acknowledge sources, tag contributors, cite inspiration. These small gestures sustain trust, the oxygen of the ecosystem. In my classroom, I reward "traceable projects", those with clear documentation of every influence.

Students learn that attribution isn't bureaucracy; its gratitude rendered visible. When people feel seen for what they've shared, they share again. That's how the loop continues.

Teaching as Infrastructure

Think of every teacher as a router in the global web of learning. Some connections are fast, others intermittent, but together they form civilization's nervous system.

Burnout is not just personal, it's systemic. When we support teachers, we maintain the network. When we encourage them to publish, post, and mentor, we strengthen the signal for everyone downstream.

The Future Bandwidth

In the coming decade, artificial intelligence, virtual labs, and augmented reality will blur the line between creator and consumer even further. The challenge won't be access to information, it'll be willingness to share it ethically.

The next generation must learn not only how to innovate, but how to contribute back. The greatest digital divide isn't connectivity; it's generosity. *

A classroom is not a container for knowledge; it's a transmitter. The signal that leaves your room, ideas, empathy, curiosity, travels farther than you'll ever see. Each student who teaches another becomes your echo in the world.

So, wire your lessons for connection. Leave ports open for collaboration.

Build bridges instead of borders. Because someday, a student you've never met will use what you shared to light another mind, and that, more than any test score, is the true bandwidth of education.

MINDSET RULE NINE
VOID WARRANTIES
VOID IF REMOVED

Mindset Rule Nine

Void Warranties

"Ownership doesn't end at the point of purchase."

The Day I Broke My First Rule (and My First TV)

It was 1975 when I voided my first warranty. I didn't call it that then, I just called it curiosity.

The family television had lost its sound, and the local repair shop wanted fifty dollars to fix it, which was about two months of lawn-mowing money. I wasn't about to pay for that.

So, I did what any determined child with a screwdriver and a death wish would do: I hooked up the TV's audio output to a pair of stereo speakers I'd salvaged from a garage sale. I figured sound was sound, how different could it be?

When the static turned into music and dialogue, I felt like I'd cracked the universe. The family wasn't as impressed. My father muttered something about "warranty voided," though in truth the TV had been broken long before I touched it.

That was the first time I realized something profound: fear is the first lock you have to pick. The second is the one held by a corporation that insists you shouldn't try.

The Fear Factory

Warranties are supposed to protect consumers from defects. Somewhere along the line, they became shackles that protect corporations from curiosity.

A single sticker, "Warranty Void if Removed", isn't just a warning label. It's psychological conditioning. It tells you that curiosity is dangerous, that ownership is conditional, that you are a user, not a maker.

That sticker is the corporate equivalent of "Don't look behind the curtain." And yet, behind that curtain is where learning happens. Every tinker, engineer, and inventor whoever changed the world ignored some version of that warning. They opened, dissected, and repurposed the tools of their time, sometimes with sparks flying, sometimes with lawsuits following.

When companies use fear and fine print to stop exploration, they're not protecting innovation; they're protecting monopoly. The fear of "breaking something" has been cultivated deliberately, and it has crippled generations of would-be makers.

The Myth of the Sticker

Let's be honest: a sticker can't revoke curiosity. In the early days of consumer electronics, those labels were meant to keep out people who might cause harm to themselves or the device. But in recent decades, they've become something else, a control mechanism.

Modern manufacturers design products that are intentionally sealed, glued, and password locked. They warn that opening them voids your warranty, as if removing a screw were an act of rebellion against civilization itself.

The truth is simpler: they don't want you to see how cheaply things are made, or how easily they could be fixed.

The "void warranty" threat isn't about quality. It's about ownership. It's a way of saying, "You paid for access, not for agency."

The Right to Repair, A Battle for Autonomy

Across the globe, the "right to repair" movement has become one of the most important civil pushes of our time. Farmers in the Midwest have discovered they can't fix their own tractors because the onboard computers are locked by digital handcuffs. Phone owners can't replace their batteries without proprietary tools. Even medical devices require company permission to service.

That's not progress; its paralysis disguised as convenience. When corporations contribute to political campaigns to criminalize self-repair, they're not protecting consumers, they're bribing the system to outlaw curiosity. The language may be legal, but the intent is moral theft.

Once you purchase something, it should belong entirely to you, body, circuit, and soul. Ownership without the freedom to alter is just rental with paperwork.

The Philosophy of Breaking Things

Every act of tinkering is, at its core, an act of philosophy. When you open a machine, you're making a declaration: I believe in my capacity to understand.

To void a warranty is to assert faith in the human mind's ability to comprehend complexity and improve it. That's not vandalism, it's enlightenment with a screwdriver. Yes, there's risk. You might destroy something expensive. You might even shock yourself. But all true learning begins with risk. You cannot separate creativity from danger any more than you can separate lightning from thunder.

The maker's path isn't about safety, it's about stewardship. The goal isn't destruction for its own sake but understanding through engagement.

If a corporation builds a device so fragile that curiosity can destroy it, that's not your fault, it's theirs.

The Malfunction Chip and the Myth of Planned Obsolescence

You've probably noticed it yourself. A device that runs perfectly for one year suddenly begins to glitch the week after the warranty expires. The refrigerator hums like a jet engine. The phone battery dies faster than a candle in a hurricane. Planned obsolescence isn't science fiction, it's business strategy.

Products are designed to fail within predictable lifespans to keep the consumer loop spinning. Repair becomes intentionally inconvenient, expensive, or "unauthorized." When repair is denied, replacement becomes the only choice. That's not just wasteful, it's predatory. The ethical maker understands this trap and steps outside it. We open, we diagnose, we learn. Each time we repair something ourselves, we reclaim a small piece of independence lost to a disposable culture.

Maker's Mindset

The Great Unlearning

There was a time when every high school in America offered shop class. Students learned to repair engines, solder circuits, and build furniture. Those programs quietly disappeared in the late twentieth century, replaced by standardized testing and career pathways designed to produce consumers, not creators.

Without hands-on education, fear took root. Children stopped learning how things work and started believing they weren't supposed to. That unlearning created a society that trades competence for convenience and autonomy for automation. The cost is cultural amnesia, we've forgotten that human progress depends on curiosity, not compliance.

Reverse Engineering as Literacy

To open a device and study its design is to read a language written in silicon and steel. Every resistor, every bracket, every welded seam tells a story about how someone solved a problem. When you reverse engineer something, you're reading that story backward, decoding intention from assembly. It's an act of respect, not rebellion. Understanding how something works doesn't diminish its creator; it honors them. The true crime is when manufacturers treat understanding as theft.

Ethics and Boundaries

Now, let's be clear: voiding warranties isn't a blank check for piracy or exploitation. There's a difference between hacking and stealing. If you bypass a lock to learn, repair, or improve something you own, you're exercising your right to explore. If you do it to exploit someone else's labor or profit from their code, you're crossing into unethical territory. The line isn't hard to see; it's drawn with intent. The maker's mindset respects creation even while deconstructing it. We disassemble to discover, not to deceive.

Tools and Freedom

When a manufacturer restricts access to repair manuals or proprietary parts, they're not protecting safety, they're protecting profit margins. But every barrier they build has an equal and opposite reaction: a generation of makers determined to tear them down. Independent repair shops, online forums, and maker communities are restoring what education and industry have lost: collective competence.

The resurgence of repair culture isn't nostalgia, it's evolution. Every tutorial uploaded to YouTube, every schematic shared on GitHub, every teacher who encourages a student to open a gadget instead of replacing it, these are quiet revolutions.

From Appliance Graveyards to Maker Havens

Visit any landfill, and you'll find the ghosts of convenience: televisions, laptops, printers, and drones, all discarded for minor faults. Each one is a story of premature death by design. Yet walk into a maker space, and you'll see resurrection. Old electronics have become robots. Broken appliances become art. Scrap metal becomes kinetic sculpture. Makers see what corporations ignore: value in the broken, potential in the obsolete. To avoid a warranty is to join that rebellion, to refuse to let waste win.

Maker's Mindset

When the Law Lags Behind the Mind

Innovation always outpaces legislation. The first people to break rules are rarely criminals; they're explorers walking faster than the map. When lawmakers criminalize self-repair at the urging of corporate donors, they're not defending justice, they're defending the status quo. The law should serve human progress, not corporate comfort. The same spirit that once made backyard scientists, garage inventors, and student engineers possible is being legislated into silence. And yet, silence never stops curiosity, it only drives it underground. Every time you open a sealed device, you're not breaking the law; you're reminding the world that progress is a natural right.

The Economic Argument for Rebellion

Repair isn't just philosophy, it's fiscal sanity. Replacing a $1,200 phone over a $40 battery is economic absurdity. Repairing it yourself is not only cheaper; it's educational. When people repair, they reduce waste, build skill, and create local jobs. Every independent technician is a node of resilience against the corporate monopoly. The right to repair isn't anti-business, it's pro-community.

The Tinkerer's Code

Every maker who opens a device inherits an unspoken code of ethics:

- If you break it, learn from it.

- If you fix it, document it.

- If you improve it, share it.

- If you borrow from others, credit them.

- If you're warned not to open it, open it anyway, but carefully.

We don't see this as recklessness; we see this as responsibility. It's how humanity advances: one cracked seal, one curious question, one rebuilt circuit at a time.

Ownership and Identity

There's a deeper psychological layer here. When you can't open what you own, you stop seeing yourself as capable. The line between user and maker blurs in favor of dependency. But when you take a screwdriver to something forbidden and make it work again, you reclaim identity. You're no longer just a consumer, you're a contributor. You stop asking permission to create. You begin to trust your own hands again. That confidence spills into every aspect of life. The courage to open a laptop leads to the courage to question authority, to challenge broken systems, to fix what others say can't be fixed. Voiding a warranty, in that sense, becomes a spiritual act, a small assertion of self-reliance in a world that profits from helplessness.

When Curiosity Becomes a Crime

Let's imagine a future, one not too distant, where unlocking a device is punishable by fine, where curiosity is "tampering," and where innovation requires licensing fees. That future already exists in fragments. It's visible in farmers forced to pirate software to repair their tractors, in smartphone users told that "opening your case may violate terms of service," in educators who can't replace batteries in district-issued laptops without corporate approval.

That's not progress, it's feudalism with Wi-Fi.

The spirit of the maker rejects that world. We void warranties because we refuse to surrender our right to wonder.

Fear as a Design Feature

Corporations learned long ago that fear is cheaper than locks. Why do you spend money on security hardware when a single label can do the job? Fear prevents you from even trying. It turns ordinary curiosity into moral hesitation.

But once you overcome that fear, once you hear the satisfying click of a screw coming loose for the first time, you realize there was never any real danger at all. Just the illusion of limitation. The moment you open something sealed; you're opening a part of yourself that's been sealed too.

Education Begins at the Screwdriver

In my classroom, the phrase "voiding warranties" isn't rebellion, it's curriculum. We collect broken devices and make them teaching tools.

Every screw removed is a lesson in mechanical literacy. Every failed repair becomes data. Every success becomes empowerment. When students realize that every product on the planet was designed by someone smarter than they are, something shifts. Fear turns into fascination. Ownership turns into understanding.

That's the mindset this rule celebrates, the courage to learn by doing, even when "doing" is discouraged.

Rebellion as Responsibility

Voiding warranties is not about chaos; it's about stewardship. It's the act of taking responsibility for what you own and what you consume. When you fix something, you extend its life and reduce its waste. When you open something, you contribute to collective knowledge. The world doesn't need more obedient consumers. It needs responsible rebels, people willing to challenge convenience culture and reclaim the dignity of competence.

If society punishes curiosity, then curiosity itself becomes the highest form of civic duty.

You can't truly own something until you understand it. A warranty is a corporate promise of safety. Curiosity is a human promise of progress. When those two collide, choose progress. Because every sealed device is a metaphor for a sealed mind, and both were made to be opened.

Maker's Mindset

Deep Dive 9.1: The Right to Repair

When ownership met resistance. A Movement Born from Frustration. Movements rarely start in boardrooms. They begin in basements, barns, and garages, where ordinary people hit a wall and refuse to stop.

The "Right to Repair" revolution began this way: with frustrated farmers staring at broken tractors they couldn't legally fix.

For decades, farmers repaired their own machines. A wrench, a socket set, and a steady hand could keep an entire farm alive. But in the early 2000s, something changed. Tractor manufacturers began installing software locks that required proprietary diagnostic codes. If a sensor malfunctioned, the entire system shut down until an authorized technician, charging hundreds per hour, arrived with a laptop and a password.

The logic was chillingly simple: control the repair, control the revenue. That was the spark that lit the fuse. From rural America to urban maker spaces, people started asking: If I buy something, do I truly own it?

The Modern Feudal System

Ownership used to be straightforward. You paid for an object, it was yours. End of story.

But in the digital age, that contract has eroded.

Corporations now sell access disguised as ownership.

You don't own your smartphone; you license the software. You don't own your car; you rent its firmware. You don't own your printer; you're renting permission to use its ink.

This model mirrors medieval feudalism more than modern capitalism. Back then, peasants worked land they could never truly claim. Today, consumers live under digital landlords who decide what's "authorized."

When companies threaten legal action against those who dare to fix, modify, or repurpose what they own, they're not protecting innovation, they're resurrecting serfdom.

Case Study: The John Deere Paradox

Few stories capture the absurdity of restricted repair like that of John Deere. Farmers who purchased their tractors for hundreds of thousands of dollars discovered that they could not legally repair them. The software running those machines was encrypted, and access required a proprietary key. The irony? The very people who grow the nation's food were locked out of their own tools. Some resorted to hacking Ukrainian firmware just to plow their fields.

John Deere claimed it was about safety and protecting "intellectual property." But the farmers knew better. It was about control, controlling who profits, who repairs, and ultimately, who depends on whom.

When a farmer can't fix his own machine, he doesn't own the land he works, he rents it from the corporation that owns the code.

Maker's Mindset

The Smartphone Dilemma

Tech companies learned the same playbook.

A simple cracked screen or dying battery became a multi-hundred-dollar affair, funneled through "authorized" repair centers that charge more for service than replacement.

For years, Apple's devices were notorious for their proprietary screws, sealed batteries, and parts that refused to work unless "activated" by company software. They warned customers that unauthorized repairs would "void the warranty." And yet, when investigative labs compared repairs from certified technicians and independent ones, they found negligible differences, sometimes even better quality from the independents.

Eventually, public pressure forced change. In 2022, Apple announced limited self-service repair programs. It was a symbolic victory but a strategic half-measure: expensive, cumbersome, and still tied to corporate approval.

The revolution had begun, but the empire wasn't surrendering easily.

Why Corporations Fear the Tinkerer

To understand corporate resistance, you have to understand fear. Manufacturers fear the chaos of creativity. They fear that someone might modify their product and expose flaws. They fear liability. They fear losing profit margins on repair monopolies. But most of all, they fear irrelevance.

If users can open, fix, and improve their own tools, the corporation loses its throne as the sole arbiter of value.

We become known as those "dangerous people with screwdrivers", is treated with suspicion. We represent autonomy, and autonomy doesn't fit neatly into business models designed around dependence.

The Locked Laptop

My school received a batch of refurbished laptops for classroom use. Within months, several began failing, bad hinges, loose screens, and swollen batteries. When we contacted the manufacturer, they quoted repair costs higher than the unit's price. Worse, they warned that opening the devices we could "violate licensing agreements."

So, we opened them anyway. We documented the process, replaced the parts, and saved thousands in budget funds. The district never reprimanded us. In fact, they started sending more devices our way for "unauthorized repairs." That's the quiet revolution, the moment when defiance becomes common sense.

When Law and Logic Diverge

The legal debate around repair isn't about right or wrong, it's about money. Corporations lobby lawmakers to maintain control under the guise of safety and quality assurance. They claim that user repairs pose risks, but what they truly fear is disruption of the service-based revenue stream. In 2018, the U.S. Supreme Court made a landmark ruling: once a product is sold, the manufacturer's patent rights are exhausted. In plain terms, when you buy it, you own it. That should have ended the argument.

Maker's Mindset

It didn't. Manufacturers simply shifted tactics, from patents to software licenses, from hardware locks to legal loopholes. The battlefield moved from the garage to the courtroom.

Europe's Example

Europe has taken a different path. The European Union's "Ecodesign Directive" mandates that appliances like washing machines and refrigerators be designed for repairability. Spare parts must be available for up to ten years.

That single law reframed design philosophy. Companies began creating modular components and publishing repair manuals again, not because they wanted to, but because they had to. It's proof that legislation can realign innovation with ethics. The U.S. will eventually follow, but the delay shows where our priorities still lie not with citizens, but with shareholders.

Repair as Civic Duty

Fixing something broken is an act of environmental and social responsibility. Each repair diverts waste from landfills, saves resources, and builds skill. Yet in a world obsessed with "new," repair is treated like rebellion.

We've been conditioned to conflate convenience with progress. But true progress isn't measured by how easily we replace; it's measured by how wisely we sustain.

When makers choose to repair rather than replace, they quietly restore balance between consumption and creativity. They remind society that sustainability begins not with recycling bins, but with screwdrivers.

The Educational Impact

In classrooms, teaching changes everything. Students who open and rebuild old hardware gain not only technical skills but moral ones: patience, accountability, and respect for design. They learn that every object embodies human effort. Every wire soldered, every joint welded, every component assembled carries intention. When a student revives a dead laptop, they're not just learning mechanics, they're learning stewardship. That's what the "Right to Repair" truly protects: the right to care.

Corporate Narratives vs. Human Truths

Corporations will continue to market "innovation" while quietly building barriers. Their advertisements show glowing hands interacting with sleek, sealed devices that promise magic at the tap of a finger. But behind that veneer lies dependency, batteries that can't be replaced, screws that strip by design, and updates that slow your system to nudge you toward the next model. The human truth is simpler: innovation that isolates isn't innovation, it's manipulation.

Technology should empower, not domesticate.

The Maker's Manifesto

The "Right to Repair" is more than policy; it's philosophy. It affirms three principles central to the Maker's Mindset: Ownership is

Maker's Mindset

Total. If you buy it, you own it. Every bolt, byte, and blueprint. Repair is Education. Fixing something is a lesson in design, patience, and independence. Curiosity is a Human Right. To deny exploration is to deny evolution. If a company's business model depends on suppressing these truths, it's not sustainable, it's parasitic.

Resistance Becomes Culture

What began as small protests in rural repair shops have grown into a global movement. Makerspaces, tech collectives, and citizen engineers now host "Repair Cafés" where volunteers teach people to fix everything from toasters to tablets. Each repaired item becomes a conversation about empowerment. Each broken hinge or cracked screen repaired without permission becomes an act of quiet revolution. This movement doesn't seek chaos. It seeks competence. It asks for nothing radical, just the right to understand, maintain, and improve what we own.

The Printer that Learned to Listen

A student once brought in a printer that refused to function because it had "reached its service life." The manufacturer embedded a counter that disabled it after a set number of pages. We found the code online, reset the counter, and printed another hundred pages. The student looked at the machine, then at me, and said, "So… it wasn't broken?" I smiled. "No. It was obedient." That day, she learned the most important lesson of all: obedience is not the same as functionality.

The Ripple Effect

Every law that changes, every repair guide released, every student who chooses to fix instead of discard adds to the momentum. As corporations double down on restrictions, makers double down on curiosity. History shows that the more power tries to centralize, the more innovation disperses. It's the law of creative thermodynamics; curiosity always finds the path of least resistance.

The Future of the Revolution

The Right to Repair movement is still in its adolescence. The next stage will go beyond access; it will demand design transparency. Imagine a world where every product ships with its schematics, where parts are modular, and where documentation is open by default. That world isn't utopia, it's simply fair. Technology once promised to democratize knowledge. The Right to Repair is how we make that promise real again.

Maker's Reflection

When corporations build walls, makers build ladders. The Right to Repair is not just about fixing objects, it's about fixing a relationship: between human curiosity and the tools we depend on. Every screw turned, every wire reconnected, every "unauthorized" act of learning is a reminder that progress doesn't need permission. The revolution is already happening. You'll hear it in every garage, classroom, and kitchen table where someone picks up a tool and whispers, "I can fix this."

In the classroom, the Right to Repair is not a political stance; it's a literacy skill. Teaching students to open, inspect, and understand the objects they use every day builds critical thinking, ethical reasoning, and confidence. The goal isn't rebellion—it's comprehension. When students learn how things are built, they learn how decisions are made, power is structured, and responsibility is shared.

Deep Dive 9.2: The Ethics of Breaking Things

Why destruction, in the right hands, becomes understanding.

The Sound of the First Snap

If you've ever taken apart a piece of technology, a phone, a controller, a remote, you know the moment. That tiny snap of plastic when the casing gives way feels both thrilling and terrifying. You've crossed a line. You're inside now.

For most people, that sound means trouble. For makers, it's the sound of possibility. But here's the paradox: to understand how something works, you must first accept that you might break it. Curiosity, by nature, is destructive. Every discovery in human history, from splitting atoms to decoding DNA, began with someone breaking something open. The ethics of breaking things begins there, at that moment when curiosity outweighs fear.

Curiosity as a Moral Act

There's a myth that curiosity is neutral, that it's neither good nor bad, only intent matters. But curiosity itself carries moral weight. To be curious is to care enough to understand. It's the opposite of apathy. It's the spark of stewardship.

When I crack open an old circuit board, I'm not vandalizing; I'm conversing with the engineer who built it. I'm asking questions across time: Why did you design it this way? What problem were you solving? What could we do better now? That's not destruction, it's dialogue. And dialogue, in the maker's world, is sacred.

Maker's Mindset

The Maker's Dilemma

There's an unspoken tension in every workshop: the balance between reverence and rebellion. On one hand, you respect the craftsmanship of the object before you. On the other, you know progress only happens when boundaries are tested. That's the maker's dilemma: How far can I go before understanding becomes arrogance?

Every act of disassembly carries a moral question:

Am I learning, or am I looting?

Am I improving, or am I imitating?

Am I experimenting, or am I exploiting?

These are not questions of law, they're questions of integrity and integrity are the only thing that separates a maker from a vandal.

Field Note: The Radio Autopsy

When I was sixteen, I salvaged a broken transistor radio from a neighbor's trash can. The casing was cracked, the dials stiff with rust. My father asked, "Why not just buy a new one?" I told him, "Because this one already knows how to sing, I just need to remind it." I disassembled it carefully, cleaned the joints, resoldered two broken traces, and replaced a corroded capacitor. When it finally came alive again, playing a fuzzy tune from the AM band, I felt something close to awe. That moment shaped how I see every object: not as property, but as partnership. The radio wasn't just mine to own; it was mine to understand.

That's the ethic of breaking things, to break with care.

Destruction as a Form of Respect

It sounds counterintuitive, but breaking something thoughtfully can be the highest form of respect. To deconstruct a machine is to acknowledge that it has something to teach you. Every unscrewed bolt, every lifted wire, every snapped seal is a sentence in an ongoing textbook written by human ingenuity.

You learn not only how things work, but why they fail and sometimes breaking something is the only way to free its potential. When you repurpose an old DVD drive into a mini-CNC or turn a broken washing machine motor into a wind turbine, you're not desecrating, you're liberating.

Intent Defines the Act

Here's the moral rule I teach students: The intent determines the integrity. If you're breaking something to steal value, you're a thief. If you're breaking something to learn, you're a maker. If you're breaking something to improve the world, you're an innovator. The tool in your hand doesn't define your character.

Your intention does.

That distinction matters now more than ever, as "hacker" has become a loaded word, associated more with cybercrime than creativity. In truth, every great advancement in science, art, and technology came from people who "hacked" the rules of their time.

Maker's Mindset

The first chemists hacked fire.

The Wright brothers hacked wind.

Tesla hacked lightning itself.

Ethical hacking isn't about violation, it's about exploration. It's the human instinct to ask, "Can this do more than it was built for?"

The Fear of Misuse

Critics of open repair argue that allowing people to modify devices invites chaos and danger. "What if someone hurts themselves?" they say. "What if someone builds something harmful?" That fear is valid but misplaced.

Knowledge doesn't create harm; apathy does. If fear of misuse were justification for restriction, we'd have banned fire, chemistry, and flight long ago. Ethical education doesn't hide tools, it teaches responsibility. The antidote to misuse is mentorship, not prohibition. You can't stop curiosity. You can only shape it.

Breaking as a Pedagogical Tool

In my classroom, we have a project called Autopsy Day. Students bring in broken or obsolete electronics and perform structured dissections. They document every part, trace every connection, and hypothesize each component's purpose. By the end of the week, they know more about design, physics, and patience than a semester of theory could teach them. Some even manage to reassemble their devices, Frankenstein creations that hum, blink, or half-function but inspire enormous pride. Every time, I remind them:

"If you understand how to break something without fear, you'll understand how to build something without limits."

The Shadow Side of Curiosity

Of course, every virtue casts a shadow. Curiosity, unchecked by empathy, becomes exploitation. History is full of innovators who built marvels but ignored morality, chemical weapons, surveillance systems, and unethical AI. This is why ethical breaking matters. The maker's curiosity must be tethered to conscience.

You can explore any frontier, but you are responsible for what you release.

Knowledge is power; conscience is direction. Without both, invention becomes arrogance.

Field Note: The Drone in the Parking Lot

One spring afternoon, a student modified a drone for extra range. He was proud, until it lost signal and crashed into a parked car. No one was hurt, but it was a sobering moment. We used it as a lesson, not a punishment.

"What went wrong?" I asked. He explained the technical side, battery weight, power ratio, but then added, "I didn't think about where it might land." That's the crux of maker ethics: thinking beyond the self. Every modification ripples outward. Every project has consequences beyond the workbench.

The Beauty of the Controlled Break

In art, there's a concept called kintsugi, the Japanese craft of repairing broken pottery with gold, highlighting the cracks rather than hiding them.

Makers practice a similar philosophy. When we break and rebuild, the scars become part of the story.

A repaired circuit carries the fingerprints of its rebirth.

A scratched chassis tells of persistence.

A once-broken tool teaches humility.

To break something intentionally, knowing you'll rebuild it better, is a quiet act of courage. It's a conversation between imperfection and improvement.

The Corporate Counter-Ethic

Manufacturers often frame all tampering as unethical, "unauthorized modification," "voided warranty," "violated terms." But that narrative is self-serving. It assumes morality resides in the contract, not the conscience.

Corporations equate compliance with virtue and curiosity with risk. That inversion of values is dangerous. It trains people to equate obedience with goodness and innovation with threat. Ethical makers reclaim that moral language. We say:

"To question is to honor the work that came before."

"To modify is to believe in progress."

"To rebuild is to participate in creation."

Destruction and Creation as Dual Forces

Every act of creation requires some form of destruction. To build a sculpture, you chisel stone. To write code, you delete errors. To build a new paradigm, you must dismantle the old one. Breaking is not the opposite of making; it's the prelude to it. The key is purpose. Break only what you intend to understand. Destroy only what you are willing to rebuild.

Field Note: The Lightbulb of Revelation

During a workshop, a student smashed a dead lightbulb by accident and froze, expecting reprimand. Instead, I said, "Good. Now look at it." We examined the filament, the vacuum seal, and the contact points. For the first time, she understood how electricity becomes illumination. The broken bulb taught more than a dozen intact ones could. When she built her first simple circuit later that semester, she called it "Version Two of the Light I Broke." Sometimes the path to wisdom is paved with shards.

Accountability: The Invisible Tool

Breaking things responsibly require one more skill, accountability. You must own the outcomes of your curiosity. If you damage something, fix it. If you improve something, document it. If you teach someone to take apart a machine, teach them to clean up afterward. This simple ethic turns chaos into discipline. It transforms curiosity from rebellion into respect.

The Maker's Compass

Every maker needs a moral compass to navigate curiosity. Mine has four cardinal directions:

North: Respect. Every design is a story; listen before you rewrite it.

Maker's Mindset

South: Responsibility. You are accountable for what you build and what you break.

East: Empathy. Every invention touch life beyond your own.

West: Wonder. Never lose the childlike joy that started all of this.

When you align your actions with that compass, breaking becomes a form of creation in disguise.

The Legacy of the Ethical Breaker

The best innovators aren't remembered for what they built, but for what they freed. They opened systems, liberated ideas, and gave others permission to explore. Ethical breaking leaves a trail of improved blueprints, cleaner code, safer devices, and wiser learners. It builds an invisible inheritance for future makers, proof that progress can coexist with integrity.

The first break is the hardest, but it's also the most honest. To break something is to admit you want to understand it. To rebuild it is to prove that you care enough to make it better. The ethics of breaking things isn't about what you destroy, it's about what you awaken: humility, curiosity, and conscience. The world doesn't need more rule-followers. It needs careful breakers; people are brave enough to open the sealed and wise enough to repair what they find inside.

Deep Dive 9.3: The Joy of the Fix

Why does repairing something broken feel like repairing yourself?

The Quiet Triumph

There's a special kind of silence that follows success, the silence after the click, the hum, the flicker of life returning to a once-dead machine. If you've ever spent hours hunching over a circuit board, soldering iron trembling slightly, then finally watched the LED blink as it was meant to, then you know the feeling. It isn't pride exactly. It's peaceful.

Repair, in its purest form, is restoration. Not just of the object, but of confidence, patience, and connection. When you fix something, you bridge the gap between failure and faith. That moment, that blink of light or spin of gears, is the maker's version of prayer answered.

The Psychology of Repair

Modern psychology tells us that repairing things provides measurable benefits to mental health. The act of restoration releases dopamine, the neurotransmitter of reward and learning. The brain recognizes completion as resolution. But beyond chemistry, repair touches something deeper: the human need to mend what's broken, both in the world and within us.

The joy of the fix is not about ownership, it's about agency. It's proof that you can confront chaos and bring order through patience, observation, and care. It's a meditation disguised as mechanics. When you repair something, you aren't just solving a problem; you're rewriting a story. You're saying, "This isn't over yet."

Maker's Mindset

The Clockmaker's Apprentice

There's an elderly man who lives two streets over from me, Mr. Garcia, a retired watchmaker. His garage is a cathedral of gears, magnifying glasses, and quiet focus. One afternoon, I visited him with an old wind-up clock I'd inherited. It hadn't ticked in years. I expected him to fix it; instead, he handed me a loupe and said, "You do it. I'll watch." It took three hours, a magnifier, and an embarrassing number of mistakes, but eventually the clock ticked again. The sound was delicate, almost shy. Mr. Garcia smiled. "You fixed time," he said. "Not bad for a beginner." I didn't just repair a clock that day. I repaired my patience. The click of each gear was a heartbeat reminding me that creation and restoration are two sides of the same craft.

The World Before "Disposable"

Once upon a time, things were built to last and built to be repaired. Every town had a cobbler, a tailor, and a radio shop. Repair was part of the rhythm of life.

When something broke, you didn't replace it, you learned about it. You gained intimacy with your possessions and, by extension, with the world. Objects weren't convenient; they were companions.

That world didn't vanish overnight. It eroded under the tide of convenience. When "disposable" became synonymous with "modern," we lost more than craftsmanship, we lost continuity. We traded sustainability for speed, and in doing so, we forgot the joy of the fix.

Repair as Resistance

Every time you choose to fix something instead of replacing it, you're defying a global narrative. You're rejecting the idea that usefulness has an expiration date. A patched jacket, a rewired lamp, a resurrected computer, they're all small acts of rebellion against a culture that profits from impermanence. Repair says, "I refuse to throw away what still has potential." And that philosophy extends far beyond objects. It's a worldview: people, communities, relationships, most things aren't truly disposable. They just need attention.

The First Fix in Every Student's Life

In every maker classroom, there's the first moment when a student fixes something broken. It's almost always accidental: a loose connection, a reversed polarity, a misaligned gear. When it works again, the look on their faces is universal, eyes wide, mouth open, disbelief melting into joy. It's the same look cave dwellers must have worn when the first fire caught. I tell them, "That's it. That's the feeling. That's the whole reason we make." Because once you've experienced the joy of bringing something back to life, it changes how you see failure forever. You stop fearing it. You start seeking it out as the doorway to understanding.

The Repairer's Mindset

Repair teaches five virtues that no textbook can:

Observation. Before you act, you must see. True repair begins with stillness and study.

Maker's Mindset

Patience. Every screw, every test, every adjustment is a meditation in restraint.

Humility. You will make mistakes. You will misdiagnose. You will learn.

Empathy. To fix something well, you must understand what it was designed to do. That requires compassion for its creator.

Hope. Every repair begins with belief that broken doesn't mean useless.

When students learn those lessons, they don't just become better engineers, they become better humans.

The Laptop Resurrection

Sometime ago, a student named Lila accidentally spilled soda on her Chromebook. The district would have charged her full replacement cost, money she didn't have. She showed up after school in tears. I handed her a small toolkit. "Let's see what's inside." She hesitated. "We'll get in trouble." "Only if we fail to learn," I said. We opened it, cleaned the board, replaced a single scorched capacitor, and reassembled it. It powered on. Lila screamed loud enough to scare the janitor. That moment didn't just save her a bill; it changed her relationship with technology. She stopped fearing machines and started mastering them.

The real warranty you earn when you void one: confidence in yourself.

The Joy of Fixing Together

Fixing alone is satisfying. Fixing together is transcendent. Community repair events, Repair Cafés, Fix-It Nights, Maker Mondays, transform isolated frustration into collective triumph. One person brings a broken blender, another brings a soldering iron, and somewhere between the laughter, the shared coffee, and the "Aha!" moments, community forms.

Repair becomes communion.

In those spaces, people rediscover what collaboration feels like when stripped of competition. No one asks for credentials. The only currency is curiosity and when the light bulb finally glows again, everyone cheers, not because the bulb matters, but because hope does.

The Spiritual Geometry of Fixing

If you pay attention, you'll notice repair follows patterns. It begins with chaos, screws scattered, wires dangling, circuits dead. Then comes order, pieces organized, faults diagnosed, structure restored. That rhythm mirrors the structure of creation itself: disorder becoming harmony through human attention. In that sense, repair is sacred geometry. It reflects our place in the universe not as consumers, but as custodians. We are not meant to leave things untouched; we are meant to touch them wisely.

The Emotional Echo of Restoration

When you fix something broken, you become part of its story. The next time you use it, you remember the problem, the process, the solution.

Maker's Mindset

You remember who helped, what you learned, how you felt. The object becomes alive again, not just mechanically, but emotionally. You no longer see a tool; you see a journey. That's why vintage instruments, heirloom furniture, and hand-repaired devices carry soul. They hold fingerprints of care, evidence that someone believed in their continued worth.

Field Note: The Toaster that Taught Gratitude

One day, my daughter asked why I kept an ancient toaster on the counter instead of buying a shiny new one. I told her the story. Years ago, it stopped working. I could have replaced it for thirty bucks. Instead, I spent an evening disassembling it, cleaning the contacts, and adjusting the thermostat. When it clicked back to life, I realized I didn't just save a toaster, I saved a habit. The habit of throwing things away too quickly. Now, every time that toaster pops, I hear a quiet reminder: gratitude hums loudest through things we've repaired ourselves.

The Repairer's Paradox

To repair something is to admit imperfection exists. To succeed is to admit that imperfection can be redeemed. That duality is the heart of the maker's philosophy. When you create something new, you're chasing potential. When you repair something old, you're honoring endurance. Both acts are essential to progress. Creation without repairing breeds' waste. Repair without creation breeds stagnation. Together, they form the complete circuit of innovation.

The Future of Fixing

As technology evolves, so will the art of repair. Future makers may use nanobots instead of soldering irons, AI diagnostics instead of intuition. But the emotional core will remain unchanged: the quiet thrill of resurrection. The coming decades will see a shift from closed systems to modular design, from proprietary secrecy to open documentation. Not because corporations suddenly grow generous, but because users demand freedom.

When people rediscover the joy of the fix, the market must follow. Demand drives ethics faster than law.

Repair as Legacy

When I look back at my life's work, it's not the polished projects that make me proud, it's the repaired ones. The machines revived from scrap, the students who discovered patience, the small triumphs that outlast their creators. Because every fix is a seed. Every repaired object extends the lifespan of knowledge.

Every person who learns to mend instead of discard becomes a guardian of sustainability. Legacy isn't what you build once, it's what you keep alive.

Maker's Reflection

Fixing things is humanity's oldest love language. Every screw tightened, every wire resoldered, every hinge adjusted says, "You still matter."

Repair is hope made visible. It's the bridge between despair and delight.

Maker's Mindset

In a world obsessed with the new, fixing something old is a radical act of faith, in skill, in patience, in the enduring worth of what we touch.

So, pick up the tool. Wipe away the dust. Breathe life into the forgotten.

The joy of the fix is not in what you restore, but in who you become while doing it.

MINDSET RULE TEN
DON'T GIVE UP

Mindset Rule Ten

Don't Give Up

DON'T EVER GIVE UP – EVER!

"Don't give in to those dark forces that rise up to oppose you. Keep pushing forward and soon you will be the success that you were meant to be."

Sadly, this is the reality that many of us face in our youth. People, especially those closest to us, tear us down. Feed us lies about ourselves without really opening up to our true potential. Falling into the darkness of despair and worthlessness seems to be the way adults address the young minds. As adults, we have forgotten the bright ideas and the shining curiosity that inhabited our youth. For many, we believe these lies to the point that we become them. "You're lazy, good for nothing, a failure, and dumb." These are just a few of the lies that were once told to me and the same lies that I hear being told to the youngest in our midst. I can only imagine that this was once an effective method for molding others into a better person, but I disagree. This author believes this is more about addressing a person's curiosity and makers desire with suppression, envy and inner anger for the lack of accomplishment from the one spewing the lies.

Keanu Reeves once said, "My biggest critics are those who have done less than I, but never more." Well, how can you apply this to a child from an adult? The older we as humans become, the more set in our ways we wallow. We as adults forget that the world is a great big universe with an untold measure of possibilities and curiosities.

Out of all the mindsets spoken at length in this book, this is the one that I have to struggle with the most. Since I was a child and more than forty years later, my ideas, thoughts and ambitions were shut down by those closest to me. It was when I was at the lowest point in my life in 1993-1994 when I just shutdown psychologically, emotionally and spiritually. I had given in to the dark forces that cascaded over me like a 360-degree tsunami washing every bit of the person I am out to sea. Even my beloved muse, the one thing I internally kept close to me was flushed. I felt broken, I felt defeated and most of all, I wanted to run. Run from my life, run from the churning vortex, I wanted to die in so many ways just to end the pain that these forced worked so hard to inflict[7].

I felt the broken pieces of me falling through a sieve as one event after another broke the remaining parts of me into smaller parts. What was left was a closed mindset that was destined to repeat the mistakes into the cycle of fights that I could not win.

Until…

Until a spark of light flashed into the darkness. Well, maybe it was not romantic, I was more of someone making it clear that I had nothing

---

[7] No, I was not suicidal. But I wanted to new identity, a new life and a fresh start.

left to lose over cold coffee (eww) and cigarettes. She (Niki Shelby) was quite correct and for some reason (now it was because she was pretty), I listened to her. I did not have to sit in darkness when I could go (metaphorically) into the light. Without revealing more, I moved to Austin Texas where I was an unknown, those dark forces would not be able to follow. To this day, those same old dark forces still reside in the land I once lived in – and that is where they will stay.

The Edge of the Cliff

Every maker, every dreamer, every person who has ever tried to create something real, eventually stands at the same invisible edge. It's the place where the excitement fades, where progress stops feeling like discovery and starts feeling like defeated. That's when the voices arrive. They don't come from outside. They come from within, quiet at first, then louder. You're not good enough. You're wasting your time. Nobody cares. Those whispers are fear made flesh. They wear the faces of critics, the echoes of parents, the sighs of bosses, and the smirks of doubters. They sound rational. They sound protective. They are liars. The first enemy you will ever meet in life is fear. And fear's greatest trick is convincing you that it's your friend.

Fear's Hidden Blueprint

Psychology tells us that fear is not weakness, it's design. The same mechanism that once kept us from walking off cliffs now stops us from sending the first email, making the first prototype, or publishing the first story. The brain treats social risk like mortal danger. It doesn't distinguish between public embarrassment and predatory threat. So, when you hesitate to share your work, when you stall mid-project, when you talk yourself out of trying, that's not laziness. That's ancient wiring. The body doesn't know you're just afraid of criticism; it thinks you're about to be eaten. But you are not a caveman anymore.

You are an architect of ideas.

You can acknowledge fear without obeying it. Because fear, once exposed to light, loses its authority. It becomes what it always was: a design flaw waiting for revision.

The Garden and the Weeds

Imagine your mind as a patch of soil. Every belief, every story you tell yourself, is a seed. Some grow into trees that shelter others. Some become weeds that strangle everything nearby. Doubt is the weed that grows fastest. It spreads through neglect. You don't have to water it; it thrives on your silence.

Every time you say, "I can't," you feed it. Every time you postpone your dream for "someday," you give it sunlight. And every time you compare your beginning to someone else's middle, you fertilize it.

The work of perseverance is not glamorous. It's gardening in the rain.

It's bending down, hands dirty, and ripping self-doubt out by the roots, again and again, until your confidence starts to bloom.

Maker's Mindset

The Skunk Sprayers

Negativity has a smell. It lingers on certain people the way burnt coffee lingers in a room long after it's gone cold. These are the skunk sprayers, the ones who cannot create, so they contaminate. They mock what they don't understand. They measure worth by conformity. They spray cynicism like perfume and call it realism.

Move upwind. You can't reason with bitterness. You can only refuse to breathe it in. Protect your work. Guard your optimism. Distance is not arrogance, it's survival. If someone consistently diminishes your fire, step away before the smoke chokes you.

The Day I Let My Muse Die

For decades I have wanted to be a writer. Long before teaching, long before engineering, it was my first love. But love can be fragile when the world teaches you to be practical. Two people I trusted ridiculed my dream. Their words were sharp and certain: "You'll never make it. You're wasting your time." I believed them. I packed away my notebooks. I buried my muse alive. For months I felt hollow. I stopped noticing beauty. I existed, but I wasn't living.

One night, unable to sleep, I turned on the radio. Bonnie Tyler's Total Eclipse of the Heart was playing. I hadn't heard it in years. Halfway through, I realized I was crying, not for what I'd lost, but for what I'd surrendered. That song woke me up. I pulled out an old notebook and wrote a single line:

"She's still in there, waiting for me to turn around." Giving up isn't the end. It's just the intermission before resurrection.

The Neuroscience of Perseverance

Psychologists describe something called "learned helplessness." It's when repeated failure conditions a person to stop trying, even when success is possible.

The gate stays open, but the mind forgets how to walk through. Every attempt you make, every time you push against the impossible, you are rewiring your brain. You're teaching it that discomfort isn't danger, it's data.

The more often you face adversity, the faster your brain recovers from it.

Resilience isn't natural, it's trained repetition. That's why we build. That's why we tinker. Every failed prototype, every burned circuit, every rejected idea is psychological exercise. You're not just making things, you're remaking yourself.

The Weight of Other People's Shadows

Some people will never support you, not because you're wrong, but because your effort exposes their inertia. Your movement makes their stillness visible. They will tell you you're unrealistic. They will label you reckless, obsessive, or naive.

Smile, thank them, and keep going. Because the moment you slow down to justify your journey to someone standing still, you've already lost momentum.

Maker's Mindset

Progress has no patience for permission.

The Lighthouse

When storms rise, and they will, look for the lighthouses: mentors, friends, teachers, stories, songs. They remind you that even in chaos, guidance exists.

But the ultimate goal is to become your own lighthouse, to stand unwavering in the tempest, shining not because the sea is calm, but because someone else might be lost. That's how endurance becomes legacy.

When you keep shining, you don't just survive, you guide.

When Compassion Turns to Self-Sacrifice

You cannot drag people out of their own darkness. You can stand beside them, you can hand them a light, but you cannot carry them up the mountain of their own making. I've seen students drown in negativity so dense it bent the air around them. They refused to see their worth even when everyone else did. I learned then that saving someone from their own despair is like swimming with a stone tied to your waist. Sometimes the most loving thing you can do is let go and focus on staying afloat.

You can't teach resilience by drowning.

The Idiot's Chessboard

There's an old saying: "Never wrestle with a pig, you both get dirty, and the pig likes it." The same principle applies to arguing with fools. A wise comedian once updated it: "Arguing with an idiot is like playing chess with a chicken, it knocks over the pieces, defecates on the board, then struts away thinking it won."

Walk away.

No maker ever changed the world by winning every argument. We change the world by building it better.

The Mountain and the Mirror

The road to mastery is not a straight line, it's a spiral staircase inside a mountain. Every revolution feels like repetition, but each loop brings you higher.

At the lowest turns, it's easy to make a mistake motion for failure. You feel like you're circling the same pain, the same doubts, the same old voices. But look closely: the view is different. That's growth.

You are not who you were the last time you faced this obstacle. You've built new clauses, new insight, new tolerance for the climb. Every step upward is invisible until you stop and look down.

The Cyclist and the Pool

Each summer I ride fifty miles to a campground. My family thinks I'm insane. They drive; I pedal. Halfway there, the wind always shifts. It pushes against me so hard I have to fight for every breath. The headwind isn't punishment, it's resistance training.

When I finally arrive, sweaty and exhausted, I find peace waiting, an empty pool reflecting a sky that doesn't care how long it took me to get there.

Maker's Mindset

That's perseverance: not speed, but endurance. The willingness to keep moving forward even when the reward seems far away and absurdly small.

Physics of Failure

Failure obeys the laws of momentum. Each attempt stores kinetic energy, experience, insight, and endurance. That energy doesn't vanish; it transfers to the next try. So, when you think you've failed completely, you haven't stopped the motion, you've only redirected it. To persist is to follow the trajectory until understanding emerges.

The Fire Theory

Fire doesn't surrender when starved of oxygen, it flickers, searching for a new source. Makers are like that. When obstacles smother us, we don't get extinguished, we adapt. You can't kill the instinct to create; you can only bury it for a while under fear, fatigue, and frustration. But creativity has a long memory. One spark, one kind word, one late-night moment of curiosity can ignite it again.

You are the fuel that keeps turning them into warmth.

The Student Who Stayed Late

Ten years ago, a seventh grader named Rina stayed after class every day for weeks. Her robot wouldn't move. She rewired it, rewrote the code, nothing worked. Finally, one evening she looked up and said, "Maybe it's me. Maybe I just can't do this."

I told her the truth: "No one can do this, until they can." She stared, blinked, and went back to work. An hour later I pointed out the simple flaw in the code. Moments after, the robot rolled forward three inches. She screamed loud enough to summon the janitor. Moments like that are what teachers live for. The sound of disbelief transforms into triumph.

The joy of the fix, the proof that persistence always whispers before it shouts.

When the World Goes Quiet

After the storm of struggle, there's a silence that feels different, not empty, but earned. You sit among your half-finished projects, your scars, your small victories, and realize you survived every catastrophe that once felt final.

Perseverance changes the architecture of the soul. You stop fearing collapse because you've learned how to rebuild.

You stop chasing validation because you've seen the light that comes only from within. You are no longer seeking the flame; you are the flame.

Becoming the Lighthouse

Someday, someone will stand where you stand now, shaken, afraid, one decision away from quitting. They'll look up and see you, still working, still standing, and realize that hope has a shape. That's the true purpose of perseverance: to turn your struggle into someone else's roadmap.

You don't just build machines or stories, you build possibility.

Maker's Mindset

The Anthem of the Unbroken

This final rule is not a command; it's a confession. I have given up before. I have surrendered to fear, to exhaustion, to the seductive ease of silence. But every time I returned, I found that the work was still waiting, patient, forgiving, eternal.

So will yours be. Don't pause for endings. Don't confuse rest with surrender.

There is no failure permanently enough to erase the act of trying again. You were born to make. That's not a hobby; it's a biological imperative. You are the descendant of those who refuse to stop. The proof of persistence written in human DNA.

Keep building. Keep breathing. Keep burning. Because the moment you stop, the world loses something it could never replace - *you*.

You will be tested by darkness not to prove its power, but to reveal your light. When the critics circle, when fatigue whispers, when the path vanishes beneath your feet, keep walking. Because the bridge you're building isn't beneath you; it's forming behind every step you take. The Maker's Mindset was never about tools or talent. It was about the will to continue.

Don't give up.

Don't dim down.

Don't let the skunks win.

You have already survived 100% of your worst days.

The next one doesn't stand a chance.

Deep Dive 10.1 – The Long Night of Duct Tape

Every maker has one, the night you almost walked away. The 2:00 A.M. Problem. Every great idea eventually hits a wall made of time, fatigue, and bad luck. For me, it was 2:00 a.m. in a classroom that smelled like solder smoke and cold pizza. The project deadline was sunrise. The robot arm, the one that had behaved perfectly for weeks, had decided to die without warning. I had three students still awake, one crying, one laughing hysterically, and one staring into the void muttering, "It was working yesterday."

Every screw stripped, every wire snapped, every bit of code refused to compile. It was the perfect storm of exhaustion and chaos. We were out of spare parts, out of time, and almost out of hope.

That's when one student said the sacred words that all makers eventually utter: "Get the duct tape." It was not elegant. It was not pretty. But the duct tape worked.

The Moment Before the Miracle

The hours before success always feel like defeat. It's that brutal psychological valley where the brain whispers, "Quit now. It'll hurt less." This is where most projects, and most dreams, die. Not in dramatic explosions, but in quiet surrender. Persistence, I've learned, begins exactly when logic gives up. It's the decision to keep moving when every cell in your body is screaming for escape.

At 3:45 a.m., we reattached the servo with a combination of tape, zip ties, and stubbornness. The arm moved, just barely, but it moved. We cheered like it had discovered fire. That's the power of duct tape: not adhesive, but attitude.

The Psychology of "One More Try"

Why do some people stop when they fail, and others keep going? Psychologists call it **grit**, the sustained effort toward a long-term goal despite adversity. Grit isn't genetic; it's cultivated. It grows every time you refuse to let defeat have the final word. Each failure you survive lowers the threshold of despair. The phrase "just one more try" is sacred. It's the incantation that turns hopelessness into momentum.

Most breakthroughs don't come from geniuses; they come from repetition.

The maker who says "one more tries" one hundred times ends up changing the world while everyone else is still complaining about why it can't be done.

The Great Melt-Down

A student named Victor once built a 3D printer from scrap. He spent weeks calibrating it, only to watch the extruder overheat and melt the print head.

The look on his face said it all, utter devastation. He wanted to quit. Instead, he took the ruined nozzle, drilled it out by hand, and rebuilt it with scavenged parts. The new design is printed cleaner than the original. Later, he taped the melted nozzle above his desk and wrote on it: "This is where I almost quit." That's the truth of every maker's journey; there's always a moment that tries to convince you to surrender. The secret is to mark that moment and keep going anyway.

The Myth of Overnight Success

Every "overnight success" story is just the final chapter of a novel written in sweat and duct tape. We love the myth because it's tidy. It spares us the ugly truth: real progress looks like failure strung together with hope. Thomas Edison failed more than a thousand times trying to invent a lightbulb. He famously said, "I didn't fail a thousand times. I discovered a thousand ways not to make a lightbulb." That's not optimism, it's engineering humor born from sleepless nights and coffee-stained notebooks.

True makers don't measure success by speed. They measure it by stubbornness.

The Fear of Looking Stupid

One of the hardest parts of not giving up is accepting that progress often looks ridiculous. You'll be the one crawling on the floor after a runaway gear while others are home watching TV. You'll be the person explaining a half-working prototype to someone who smirks and says, "That's cute."

Let them smirk. The willingness to look foolish is the down payment on innovation. Every masterpiece looks like a mess halfway through. Every hero looks like a fool right before the breakthrough. That's the moment to double down. That's the moment to tape the whole thing together and dare it fail again.

Maker's Mindset

Engineering of Emotion

Desperation has an anatomy: First comes denial ("Maybe it's just a glitch"), then frustration ("Why won't this work?"), then despair ("I can't do this"), and finally, resolve ("Fine. I'll fix it myself.")

That last stage, resolve, is where greatness begins. When you hit that emotional bottom, you have stripped away ego, excuses, and expectation. What's left is pure drive. You stop chasing perfection and start chasing progress. You stop fearing judgment and start experimenting freely. That's when miracles happen, when you stop performing for the world and start building for the love of creation itself.

The Maker's Heartbeat

At 4:15 a.m., the robot arm completed its first full motion. It waved. We burst out laughing, not because it was perfect, but because it worked. Somewhere in the sound of servo motors and duct-taped joints, we heard the heartbeat of the maker's spirit: clumsy, loud, persistent, alive. That moment didn't win an award or make the news. It didn't even earn extra credit. But I knew those students would remember it forever. They had faced failure and refused to let it win. We became unstoppable, not when we succeed, but when we realize we don't need success to keep going.

The Maker's Law of Duct Tape

If it's broken, fix it.

If you can't fix it, improvise.

If you can't improvise, adapt.

If you can't adapt, rest, and then try again. Duct tape isn't just material; it's philosophy. It represents the refusal to accept that something is permanently broken. It's the physical manifestation of hope. A small, silver roll of possibility.

Every time you patch a crack or hold two misaligned pieces together, you're saying, "This story isn't over yet."

The Long Night in Every Life

Not every long night happens in a classroom. Sometimes it happens in the quiet of your own mind, when failure isn't mechanical but emotional. When you've poured everything into a dream and all that's left is silence. Those are the nights when you discover who you really are. Not the version that looks good on paper, not the confident persona others see, but the raw, unedited you, the one who still believes even when belief hurts.

That version of you is the reason humanity has climbed mountains, crossed oceans, cured diseases, and reached the stars. That version of you is the maker's soul. And the only way to meet it is to stay awake through the long night.

Morning Comes Anyway

At 6:10 a.m., sunlight crept across the workshop floor. The robot arm sat on the table, still held together by duct tape, still wobbling, but alive. It wasn't perfect. Neither were we. But it worked long enough for a demonstration and a round of exhausted applause.

Maker's Mindset

We learned something that morning: dawn doesn't care if you finished or not, it arrives regardless. You can meet it with regret, or you can meet it with satisfaction that you gave everything you had. The sun rises either way. The only variable is how you face it.

The Physics of Persistence

Persistence is not linear. It oscillates. You'll have nights of rage followed by mornings of clarity. You'll make three steps forward and two back. You'll fail in spectacular new ways and find out that failure is, in fact, data. But every time you return to the workbench, you accumulate momentum. Even despair can be repurposed into driving if you refuse to leave it idle. That's the alchemy of the maker: turning exhaustion into endurance, turning frustration into fuel.

The Echo of Victory

A month after that sleepless night, the students brought the robot arm to a local maker fair. It shook hands with visitors and wrote "NEVER GIVE UP" on a whiteboard. People laughed, applauded, and took photos. None of them saw the duct tape holding its elbow together. They saw only the miracle. And that's the secret; the world rarely remembers the long nights. It remembers the results.

So, when you're in your own dark hour, knee-deep in mistakes, covered in metaphorical duct tape, remember this is the part of the story that nobody sees, but it's the most important part. Because without the long night, there is no sunrise.

Every long night has a sunrise waiting for it. Duct tape isn't pretty, but neither is persistence. Both hold the world together in ways perfection never could. When everything falls apart, when the wires burn out, the code collapses, the hope flickers, don't quit. Tape it, tie it, rebuild it, believe again. Because one day, that wobbling creation will move, and you'll realize it wasn't the machine you saved, it was yourself.

Maker's Mindset

Deep Dive 10.2: Psychology of Why We Do Dumb Things

Because persistence and stupidity sometimes share the same toolbox.

The Repeat Offender's Club

If perseverance had a support group, the first meeting would sound like this:

"Hi, my name is Alex, and I tried the same thing seventeen times expecting different results."

"Welcome, Alex."

We've all been there, staring at a machine, a code error, or a life choice that clearly isn't working, muttering, maybe this time it'll magically fix itself.'

It rarely does. But somehow, trying again feels safer than admitting defeat. Humans are serial experimenters trapped in emotional feedback loops. Psychologists call this reinforcement learning rogue: the brain keeps pulling the lever because sometimes, just sometimes, it gets a pellet of success.

That intermittent reward is addictive. It's why slot machines, bad relationships, and broken prototypes all keep us coming back.

The Brain, the Lab Rat, and the Loop

Neuroscience explains our irrational perseverance in one word: dopamine.

When you almost solve a problem, your brain releases a small hit of it.

That chemical whisper says, "You're close, try again." So, you do. And fail.

And try again. And fail. And suddenly it's 3 a.m. and you're bargaining with an inanimate object like it owes you rent.

The same loop powers learning, art, engineering, and questionable life decisions. The difference between a genius and a fool isn't intelligence, it's documentation.

One writes a paper about the experiment; the other repeats it next weekend.

The Solder Saga

During a robotics club building, one student kept burning the same connector. Three tries, three smoking disasters.

"Why do you keep doing that?" I asked.

He shrugged. "Because it should work."

That line should be engraved on every maker's tombstone.

"Because it should work." Logic says stop. Hope says maybe. And between those two voices lives the beautiful madness of invention.

Hope and Its Evil Twin Denial

Hope and denial are twins separated at birth. One builds bridges; the other insists the bridge is fine as it collapses. Psychology calls this optimism bias: the tendency to believe our next attempt will defy statistical probability. But here's the twist, without that bias, humanity would still be hiding in caves. We persist not because logic says yes, but because imagination refuses to accept no. That's why we rebuild civilizations after earthquakes, rewrite code after crashes, and go back to love after heartbreak.

Maker's Mindset

We keep doing "dumb" things because somewhere deep down, we know progress depends on it.

The Safety Illusion

Fear of failure often disguises itself as caution: "I'm just being realistic."

But realists rarely change the world; they just explain why it can't be changed.

To evolve, we must occasionally out stubborn our own common sense. Every invention that mattered looked irrational at first: heavier-than-air flight, electricity, vaccines, personal computers, online dating. Each began with someone saying, "This is ridiculous," and another replying, "Good, let's try it anyway."

I call this mental gear the **Maker Override**. It's the switch that flips when reason steps aside and curiosity grabs the wheel.

The Law of Creative Gravity

Anything built will eventually fail toward its weakest point. That's gravity's opinion on ambition. Our dumb persistence is the counterforce, equal, opposite, essential. You fall; you learn the angle of descent. You patch; you reinforce. Repeat enough times, and gravity becomes your teacher instead of your enemy. Every "dumb" repetition is a rehearsal for mastery. The trick is to learn faster than you break things.

The Fan Blade Incident

I once decided to balance a fan blade "by feel." Physics objected. Loudly.

The fan self-destructed, launching parts across the garage like shrapnel from a small war. My wife opened the door, surveyed the scene, and asked the only reasonable question:

"Did you learn anything?"

"Yes," I said. "That I should write this down before I try again." Documentation: the thin line between research and comedy.

Dumb Doesn't Mean Defective

We equate mistakes with stupidity, but they're different species. Stupidity repeats without reflection. Persistence experiments within failure.

When we keep doing "dumb" things, we're often stress-testing reality.

The Wright brothers crashed because air density is unforgiving, not because they lacked intelligence. Edison burned filaments because he was exploring the material limits of the universe. True idiocy is never questioning your results. True progress is questioning everything, especially yourself, and still returning to the lab tomorrow.

Why We Sabotage Ourselves

Self-sabotage often masquerades as comfort. We procrastinate, over-research, or start ten projects at once to avoid finishing the one that scares us most. It's not laziness, it's self-protection. Completion invites judgment; incompletion preserves potential. The cure is exposure therapy:

finish anyway.

Ship the imperfect prototype. Publish a messy story. Present the clunky demo.

The moment you release it, fear loses leverage. Nothing terrifies perfectionism more than motion.

Humor as Armor

When nothing works, laughter is the duct tape for the soul. It breaks the feedback loop of frustration, resets the nervous system, and reminds us that failure isn't fatal, it's just funny with bad timing. That's why makers tell horror stories like stand-up comics. If you can laugh at the explosion, you've already turned pain into data. And data, unlike despair, is reusable.

The Chicken and the Chessboard Revisited

Remember the idiot's chessboard from the core rule? Sometimes the chicken isn't a person, it's our own ego. We set up the board, knock over the pieces, curse the universe, and then strut around pretending to be victorious.

That's fine, as long as you eventually clean the board and start again.

Self-mockery is a sign of growth. The day you can laugh at your old failures without flinching is the day they stop owning you.

The Reversed Polarity Parade

In a student build contest, one team wired every LED backward. When they powered up, nothing happened, except smoke. The team laughed, grabbed the fire extinguisher, and yelled, "Prototype #2!" They finished dead last in judging but first in spirit. A year later, every member was leading new teams.

Failure had become fuel. That's the hidden math of persistence:

Every defeat compound into experience.

Every repetition refines instinct.

Every burned board becomes a boundary line you'll never cross again.

The Neuroscience of Second Chances

Brain imaging shows that learning peaks right after mistakes. The error itself triggers neuroplasticity; your brain literally rewires to avoid repeating it.

So the moment you mess up is biologically the best moment to keep going.

Giving up right then is like closing the textbook mid-highlight.

Persistence isn't defiance of biology; it's cooperation with it.

Dumb Faith vs. Smart Fear

Smart fear says, "That's unsafe."

Dumb fear says, "That's unfamiliar."

Both feel the same, but one keeps you alive and the other keeps you ordinary. The trick is discernment.

Ask yourself: Is this danger, or discomfort?

If it's discomfort, push through. Growth hides behind it.

If it's danger, get goggles. Then push through carefully.

Maker's Mindset

When to Stop

Not giving up doesn't mean never stopping. Sometimes persistence becomes obsession, and obsession eats perspective. The ethical maker knows when to pause, sleep, or start fresh. Stopping is not quitting; it's resetting the operating system. Even machines need cooldown cycles. So do we.

Maker's Mantra: Fail Responsibly, Repeat Joyfully

Write it on your bench, carve it on your mind:

"I will fail responsibly and repeat joyfully."

That's how you transform dumb persistence into disciplined resilience. You'll still make spectacular mistakes, just more efficiently, with better stories to tell.

The Final Laugh

Look back at every disaster that taught you something vital: the melted plastic, the corrupted code, the public flop that became folklore. Those weren't failures; they were field research for your future self. The human species survives because we are willing to look ridiculous on the way to brilliance. We fall, we tinker, we rebuild, we share the meme. So yes, you will keep doing dumb things.

Do them with purpose. Do them with humor. Do them with heart.

Because the line between foolishness and faith is drawn only by those who never tried.

Persistence looks dumb until it works, then it looks genius. Laugh when it breaks. Learn when it burns. Try again not because it's logical, but because it's human.

We keep doing "dumb" things because the universe rewards motion over perfection.

Keep moving, keep experimenting, and someday the world will call your stubbornness innovation.

Maker's Mindset

Deep Dive 10.3, The Bloopers Department

Because every masterpiece is built on a mountain of misfires.

The Reel That Nobody Shows

Every polished success you see, every viral invention, every beautiful prototype, has a blooper reel that never makes the presentation. The miswired breadboards. The printers that jammed mid-demo. The version of the code that caused sparks to shoot sideways instead of forward. We hide these moments like they're shameful. But the truth is, bloopers are the most honest part of creation. They're where the learning hides. They're where humanity is.

If you want to understand a maker, don't look at their final design, look at their trash bin. That's where courage lives.

Outtakes from the Workshop

Every semester I start with a simple statement: "Something in here will fail spectacularly, and that's the good part." The students laugh nervously. They think I'm joking. Then we begin building.

The failures arrive like clockwork. Screws fall into unreachable cavities. Code loops into infinity. 3D printers build abstract art that was supposed to be gears. And right when frustration peaks, laughter usually follows. Someone cracks a joke, someone else declares the failure "modern sculpture," and the room relaxes again. That's when real learning begins, when we stop hiding the mistakes and start owning them.

The Science of the Blooper

There's solid psychology behind this joy. Laughter after failure resets the stress cycle. It releases endorphins that reframe catastrophe as comedy. That neurological reset keeps curiosity alive. It gives permission to keep trying.

Without humor, failure feels fatal. With humor, it becomes fuel. That's why the most creative people you'll ever meet are also the funniest. They've learned to survive disaster with grace, and punchlines.

Field Note: The Self-Destructing Drone

Once, a team built a small drone to drop water balloons during a school fair. During the first test flight, it rose ten feet, banked gracefully, and then exploded midair. The payload detonated early, showering everyone with water.

Silence.

Then laughter.

The team bowed theatrically and yelled, "Version Two launches tomorrow!" That phrase became legend.

"Version Two launches tomorrow" turned into our shorthand for resilience. Whenever something failed after that, someone would shout it, and the tension would vanish.

It's hard to fear failure when it's part of the culture's comedy.

Why Perfection Is Boring

Perfection is static. It's beautiful, maybe, but lifeless. You can admire it, but you can't grow from it. Bloopers, on the other hand, are alive. They are moving. They teach. They remind us that creation is a living process, not a frozen ideal.

Every failure carries fingerprints, evidence of a human who cared enough to try.

When you remove the errors, you erase the evidence of courage.

The Myth of the Genius

The world loves the idea of the flawless genius, the artist who never doubts, the engineer who never miscalculates, the inventor who wakes up with perfect blueprints. But every real maker knows the truth: genius is just persistence with better notetaking. Einstein filled notebooks with dead ends. Da Vinci wrote pages of failed sketches. Even NASA, with all its rigor, runs a "Lessons Learned" database, a polite term for the Bloopers Department of Space Exploration. The only difference between a genius and everyone else is that geniuses write down their mistakes before repeating them.

Humor as an Engineering Tool

Comedy is an essential part of creative engineering. A good laugh disarms ego, invites feedback, and keeps the group cohesive through chaos. I once watched two students argue over wiring polarity until one finally said, "Let's ask the LED, it's dying to tell us." They both cracked up and solved the problem in minutes. Humor reopens the mind that frustration has closed. I tell my classes: "If you can't fix it, make it funny." Because laughing might be the spark that leads to the actual fix.

The Emotional Cost of Hiding Mistakes

When we hide every misstep, we teach others that success is effortless, and they feel broken when theirs isn't. That illusion kills creativity faster than failure ever could. Perfectionism is contagious, but so is authenticity. When one person admits, "I messed this up spectacularly," the whole room exhales. That breath is liberation. It says, "We're allowed to be human again."

The Egg Drop Debacle

When I practiced and instructed in Science, I would assign a physics challenge: protect an egg dropped from ten feet.

Most survive. Some don't.

One team forgot to tape the parachute into the container. The egg soared proudly for three seconds before becoming an omelet on impact. They stared in horror, then burst into applause. Later, they wrote in their reflection:

"We failed so hard that we stopped being afraid of failing and got an A for our explanation." That's the power of the blooper; it makes courage contagious.

The Museum of Broken Things

If I ever open a makerspace museum, half of it will be failures: cracked prints, melted circuits, snapped bolts, and burnt breadboards. Each will have a tag describing not the mistake, but the lesson. Failure deserves a gallery, not a garbage bin. Because failure is the blueprint of progress. Every broken piece carried hope. Every repair carried growth. A museum of broken things is really a museum of resilience.

The Blooper Reel of Life

Life itself is one long experiment in trial and error. We get some designs right, most wrong, and we never stop iterating. The relationships that fall apart, the jobs that implode, the ambitions that stall, all part of the reel. You can't edit them out without erasing your evolution. Laugh at them. Learn from them. Love them for what they taught you about yourself. They're not the outtakes; they're the evidence that you stayed in the story.

The Blooper Effect on Leadership

In teams, leaders who admit their own bloopers inspire loyalty. When a teacher says, "I messed that up," students feel safe to experiment. When a boss laughs at their own blunder, the whole team relaxes. That transparency transforms failure from shame to shared experience. It's not weakness, it's wisdom. You can't teach resilience from a pedestal. You teach it from the mess on the floor.

Humor and Healing

Laughter doesn't just soften the blow; it literally heals. Studies show that humor lowers cortisol levels, strengthens immune response, and increases creative problem-solving. In short: a good laugh makes you smarter.

So the next time something breaks, remember, your best repair tool might be your sense of humor.

The Student Who Fell Off the Stage

During a school presentation, a student stepped backward off a low stage while holding his project. The audience gasped. The student popped back up, raised the device overhead, and shouted, "It still works!" The crowd roared. That moment turned a potential embarrassment into legend. The student later told me, "I stopped being scared of mistakes that day." That's the graduation we're all working toward; the day fear loses its punchline.

The Laws of the Blooperverse

Every maker has a blooper reel. If they deny it, they're editing. Laughter is the best lubricant. It keeps the gears of collaboration turning. Failure shared is failure halved. Shame evaporates in daylight. A broken thing is just a future story.

Perfection is not the goal; progress is. Write those on the wall. Live by them. Add new laws as you go.

Why We Laugh at Ourselves

Because we remember.

We remember being children who built cardboard castles that collapsed five minutes later, and still called it victory. Laughter reconnects us with that fearless version of ourselves, the one who built for joy, not approval.

The adult maker spends a lifetime trying to return to that state of play.

Laughter is the bridge.

Maker's Mindset

The Circuit of Redemption

My favorite project ever built was also my biggest mess. A handmade signboard that was supposed to light up the words "STAY CURIOUS." It never worked right, half the letters flickered, the wiring looked like spaghetti. But when I flipped the switch during open house, the room went dark, one bulb popped, and the remaining letters spelled "STAY US." Everyone laughed.

I left it that way. It reminded me that perfection was never the point, connection was. People didn't remember the glitch. They remembered the laughter that followed. That's the heartbeat of the Maker's Mindset: stay human, stay trying, stay us.

The Blooper Department's Real Job

The true role of the Bloopers Department isn't to collect errors, it's to remind us why we started creating in the first place. We build not for applause, but for expression. We make it because we need to translate thought into form, and that process will always be messy.

Perfection is sterile.

Mess is life.

And laughter is the proof that life still matters more than control.

Failure is just comedy waiting for courage. Laugh loudly. Share generously. Keep your blooper reel visible, it's your real résumé.

When others see your cracks, they'll recognize their own, and together you'll discover that resilience is funnier than fear. Every misstep is a rehearsal for brilliance. Every error a wink from the universe saying,

"You're still in the game."

So, make mistakes spectacularly. Film them, name them, celebrate them.

Because someday, when success finally arrives, you'll know exactly who

earned it,

the fool is brave enough to keep laughing while building in the dark.

The Maker's Mindset Is a System

By now, it should be clear that the Maker's Mindset isn't a list of ten independent rules to memorize and follow one at a time. It's a system, interconnected, responsive, and only as strong as its weakest point of neglect.

Each rule supports the others. Safety allows experimentation. Tools extend intent. Acceptance enables collaboration. Reflection converts experience into wisdom. Community multiplies effort. When one of these is ignored, the strain shows up elsewhere. Teams grow quiet. Tools sit unused. Mistakes repeat. Progress slows. Not because people became less capable, but because the system lost balance.

Most breakdowns don't happen all at once. They begin subtly. A moment of silence instead of speaking up. A shortcut taken without reflection. A tool avoided because failure feels risky. Over time, these small fractures accumulate until the structure no longer holds under pressure.

Fear doesn't remove tools from the system. It convinces people not to reach them.

Fear is usually the force behind that erosion. Fear doesn't announce itself as panic. It shows up as hesitation, defensiveness, and disengagement. It convinces capable people to stop asking questions, to stop sharing ideas, to stop trusting the process. Left unchecked, fear doesn't just slow a system, it quietly dismantles it.

The Maker's Mindset doesn't eliminate fear. It designs around it.

- Safety interrupts panic.

- Reflection restores clarity.

- Acceptance rebuilds trust.

- Shared responsibility distributes awareness.

This is what it looks like when a system protects itself. When one voice speaks, the whole structure responds When these elements work together, fear loses its leverage. Not because it disappears, but because it no longer controls behavior.

This is why the mindset matters more than any single tool, technology, or technique. Tools will change. Environments will shift. New challenges will emerge. But a well-tuned system adapts. It learns. It recovers.

That is the real promise of the Maker's Mindset, not perfection, not certainty, but resilience. The ability to build, break, learn, and build again without losing curiosity, trust, or humanity in the process.

"Everything that follows is an invitation to put that system into motion."

I truly hope that you enjoyed this book.

Maker's Mindset

You're almost there....

...Or have you just begun?

THE CREATIVE MINDSET

About the Author

Nice to meet you dear reader. I am Thomas Burbridge (Tom), and I don't just teach engineering, I live it. A Navy veteran, lifelong tinkerer, and classroom experimenter, I believe the best lessons happen somewhere between "Oops" and "Aha!"

After ten years in the U.S. Navy and more than a decade teaching technology and robotics, I've learned that creativity isn't a gift, it's a muscle. My students (Eriks, Macey's, Juliets, Micheals and Matthews, Masons, Melas, and the thousand others) know me as the teacher who turns mistakes into momentum and failure into the funniest part of the story.

When I am not writing about creative chaos or coaxing life out of a cross wired robot, cycling Texas backroads or diving the Gulf of MEXICO just to see what's under the next wave.

For this project, I write to remind makers of every age that curiosity is a survival skill, laughter is a repair tool, and persistence is humanity's greatest invention.

Returning to graduate school in the Fall of 2019, I had no thought about compiling this into a single volume. What he did however was leverage chapters in this book as part of my assigned work papers. Perhaps you will spot areas where he had to explain some of the approaches. Still, I felt that I had something of value here.

If you're wondering what to do next, start small. Fix one broken thing. Share one idea freely. Teach one lesson you learned the hard way. You don't need permission, funding, or perfect conditions. You just need to begin. Makers don't wait for the world to change—they build the version they want to live in.

Update: The first print of this book was not supposed to be released to the world. For that I take on all the blame for the premature release.

Contact me through BeardIron Books for comments, cheers, jeers or for an autographed copy.

Accolades and Thanks

Assembling my notes, I began to compile and rewrite this book (for the 52nd time) at the following locations in Pflugerville Texas

El Rincon Mexican Restaurant

West Pecan Coffee

I deeply appreciate the patience you showed me while taking up space in your businesses while I scratched this book out by hand.

Rey Flores – Who taught me that Education is a mindset first and foremost.

Laura Brown - *psst. * Don't tell her that I think she is an outstanding leader.

Tom Ouellette – Whose BBQ trailer he built was more than just a Swiss Army Knife with hot & cold running water and 120VAC via solar power.

My son Thomas – Who I thought of when I developed these mindsets.

My clown child Emma – Passing from us into the night, I still remember your laughter when you kicked my graded assignment box over.

For my late parents – whom I began this book before they passed.

Hannabee – Thank you for your tireless work.

Russ Somers – Perhaps the most intelligent man I know.

Mark Decker – A man of many stories and great ingenuity

You are all the best!

www.ingramcontent.com/pod-product-compliance
Lightning Source LLC
Chambersburg PA
CBHW060155120726
48004CB00007B/1552